DEBRA OSWALD is a writer for stage, film, television and children's fiction.

Her stage plays have been produced around Australia. *Gary's House*, *Sweet Road* and *The Peach Season* were all shortlisted for the NSW Premier's Award. Her play *Dags* has had many Australian productions and has been published and performed in Britain and the United States. *Gary's House* has been on the senior high school syllabus, and has been performed in translation in both Denmark and Japan. *The Peach Season* won the 2005 Seaborn Playwright's Prize. *Mr Bailey's Minder* broke the Griffin Theatre's box office record in 2004, toured nationally in 2006, and was produced in Philadelphia in 2008.

Debra has written two plays for the Australian Theatre for Young People. *Skate* was performed in Sydney, on a NSW country tour and at the Belfast Theatre Festival. *Stories in the Dark* premiered at Riverside Theatre Parramatta in 2007.

She is the author of three 'Aussie Bite' books for kids, including *Nathan and the Ice Rockets*, and five novels for teenage readers: *Me and Barry Terrific*, *The Return of the Baked Bean*, *The Fifth Quest*, *The Redback Leftovers* and *Getting Air*.

Among Debra's television credits are *Bananas in Pyjamas*, *Sweet and Sour*, *Palace of Dreams*, *The Secret Life of Us* and award-winning episodes of *Police Rescue*.

Shane Connor as Gary in the 1996 Playbox Theatre Centre / Q Theatre production. (Photo: Geoff Beatty)

Gary's House

DEBRA OSWALD

Currency Press ◆ Sydney

CURRENCY PLAYS
Gary's House first published in 1996
by Currency Press Pty Ltd,
PO Box 2287, Strawberry Hills NSW 2012 Australia
enquiries@currency.com.au
www.currency.com.au
Revised edition published 2000
Reprinted 2000, 2003, 2004, 2009

NATIONAL LIBRARY OF AUSTRALIA CIP DATA
 Oswald, Debra.
  Gary's house.
  ISBN 978 0 86819 607 7.
  I. Title.
  A822.3

Cover design by Kate Florance
Cover photograph shows Shane Connor as Gary in the 1996 Playbox
Theatre Centre / Q Theatre production. (Photo: Geoff Beatty)
Set by Dean Nottle

Contents

Currency Press acknowledges the Traditional Owners of the Country on which we live and work. We pay our respects to all Aboriginal and Torres Strait Islander Elders, past and present.

For Gillian Higginson

Two Worlds

John McCallum

'Please stay!' people keep begging each other in what becomes a refrain in this bittersweet play. A ratbag collection of misfits, loners, drifters and losers are thrown together on a scrubby patch of remote bush—loosely united in a comically desperate project, which we watch on stage, to build Gary's house.

The house—the raising of its frame, the cladding of its walls, the lighting of its windows and the final ritual of the opening of its front door—is a real object constructed in front of us. Gary starts it and it is a solid metaphor—one you can walk through once you've built it and lock up against the world—for the chaotic struggle that people face as they try to build quiet lives for themselves

The play is about a battling underclass of suffering-but-resilient people thrown back on their own resources by a new, coldly executive, society that sacrifices human lives for the sake of sound management and efficient social control.

The characters keep leaving each other, as they struggle to go it alone, but then they keep coming back together again and finding, in their different idiosyncratic ways, a sense of community. Outcast people, the play suggests, sometimes manage to find each other and to battle on.

Gary and Sue-Anne aren't up to much, and they know it. He is full of pent-up violence and barely controlled anger which something in him wants to control and channel into the building of his house. She has the self-absorption, comically expressed, of the powerless unloved, scarcely able to comprehend the material support, born of inarticulate love, that people like Gary have to offer. They are an unlikely couple—she with her bag full of empty

Violet Crumble Bar wrappers and he with his bag full of nails—but somehow they have managed, so far, to muck along.

They first met in a scenario written for them not by a Mills and Boon writer but by the hard-nosed lawyers and accountants who employed him to check up on her to see if she was cheating on her workers' compensation claim. She wasn't (she wouldn't know how) but she thought he was cute when she found him parked outside her house in his little van. ('The most pissweak spy', she says happily.) Now he is building a house, in which to raise a baby, on a block of land he only half owns, without plans, for a woman he only half knows.

As a couple they are, to use the current euphemism for people whom society has failed, dysfunctional. Their crazy relationship is the emotional core of the first half of the play, but under pressure they don't stay with each other. Sue-Anne leaves Gary because she doubts his ability to deliver his dream, and Gary suddenly and dramatically leaves Sue-Anne at the end of Act One by shooting himself. Both actions are failures of love and hope, on the part of people who have never had any public or private model for either, but who for a brief cheerful time had something else to be going on with.

The other great pair in the play, who play out a sort of comic subplot, are Christine, Gary's alienated sister, and Dave, the laconic, laidback loner camped in his dead father's burnt-out house next door. Christine has spent her life working desperately hard at her career, becoming a superbitch, and keeping her fears at bay. Dave loves work so much that he can sit and watch it for hours. They are another unlikely couple, and their surprisingly abrupt coming together is the emotional core of the second half.

They are the outsiders who hang in there, the drifters who finally stick. Early in their prickly relationship Christine asks Dave to stay for just one night, but he won't. For most of the play he seems to be waiting for his chance to leave, but gradually we realise that he is never going to.

Vince, the weedy little bloke from the shop in town, seems to be terminally scared of everyone and everything, but in his odd way he proves loyal and strong at the end as he devotedly takes on the terrible burden of loving Sue-Anne.

In the weary but warm resolution to this play we are confronted, shockingly, with two relationships that just might last.

We are also confronted, in the final minutes, with the even more shocking (for some of the critics, at least) moment of silent communion between the ghost of dead Gary and the newly alive Christine.

Christine has learnt, after all the cynicism and self-doubt that she has been nurturing in herself, to cherish the smell of a baby. She has had one herself by this stage. In the last scene she takes up Sue-Anne and Gary's crying son and carries him upstage to the threshold of the house that she has finished building for her dead brother. Gary himself appears in the doorway, and takes the baby, who is suddenly quiet.

It is an overtly theatrical moment, at the end of a realistic play. It suggests that there are values that transcend the simple selfish claims of the individual. Suddenly, in an emotionally explosive ending, two people and their two worlds come together.

John McCallum

Gary's House was first produced by Playbox Theatre Centre, Melbourne, and the Q Theatre, Penrith, on 1 March 1996, with the following cast:

GARY	Shane Connor
DAVE	Terence Crawford
SUE-ANNE	Sophie Lee
CHRISTINE	Ailsa Piper
VINCE	Conrad Page

Director, Kim Durban
Designer, Judith Hoddinott
Lighting Designer, Andrew Kinch

CHARACTERS

GARY
DAVE
SUE-ANNE
CHRISTINE
VINCE

SETTING

A house-building site on a remote bush block.

ACT ONE

SCENE ONE

A building site on a remote bush block. We can see the brick footings of a small house. The site is strewn with tools, piles of bricks and general building debris. GARY *is working on the site, hammering down sheets of flooring onto the brick footings. He calls to the campsite offstage.*

GARY: Bring us the water bag, will ya?

> *There's no answer.*

You hear me, Sue-Anne?

> *Still no answer from the campsite.*

Get out here now! I'm not mucking 'round.

> *Finally, he hurls the hammer down and stalks towards the campsite, winding himself up into a stiff-necked rage.*

Sue-Anne!

> *On the way, he reaches down and snatches up a cheap Indian cloth shoulder bag. All he unearths from the bag is a fistful of Violet Crumble wrappers. This seems to wind him up even further until the sinews in his neck are snapped tight. The rage overtakes* GARY *physically, like a fit that he's accustomed to handling.*

Jesus, Sue-Anne! Jesus H. Christ!

> *He stabs his head against the air, arms jerking to stop himself punching at nothing. He circles, trying to absorb the anger in constant movement. Finally he stops, sucking in short, sharp breaths. He consciously places his body in a controlled posture, to make his body act out the movements of a calm and reasonable person. He walks back to the footings. He starts nailing again, attacking the task fiercely, pushing the*

rage into each swing of the job. The rage subsides gradually. He sees someone walking up the slope towards the building site. GARY *nods in greeting. His manner with* DAVE *is very guarded.*

G'day.

DAVE *doesn't hurry the last few metres up to where* GARY *is working. But he flashes* GARY *a killer smile, laid-back and matey.* DAVE *is in his late thirties. He has cultivated an easygoing, larrikin charm that has served him well. He's profoundly lazy, resolutely an observer, but still manages to seem like a lively, buoyant person.* DAVE*'s got the gift of adjusting his style just enough to suit whoever he's with and getting people talking.*

DAVE: G'day. I'm Dave.

GARY: Gary.

DAVE: You'll kill yourself, mate—working like that in the heat of the day.

GARY: Got no choice. Gotta get it finished in time.

DAVE: Fair enough.

DAVE *eases himself down to sprawl on the ground near where* GARY*'s working.*

Heard about you down at the pub. Thought I'd come over and check out how you're going.

GARY *hesitates, seeing this bloke settle in for a long stay.*

Don't slow down because of me. I don't mind if you keep working.

GARY *gets back into work, wary of this guy's motives.*

GARY: You didn't see a red ute along that road, did ya?

DAVE *shakes his head, grinning. He watches* GARY *work.*

DAVE: What—you're doing a pine frame, zincalume roof? What's your cladding?

GARY: Hardiplank.

DAVE: Good idea. Goes up very easy that stuff.

GARY: You in the building trade, are ya?

DAVE: [*with a dazzling grin*] Ooh no, mate. Too much hard slog in building.

> DAVE *relaxes into comfortable silence. But* GARY *isn't comfortable.*

GARY: Live 'round here, do ya?

DAVE: [*shaking his head*] Grew up here though. Next door.

GARY: The place that burnt down?

DAVE: Yeah.

GARY: You taking over the place?

DAVE: [*laughing*] Shit, no. Nah... I'm just here to sort out legal stuff on the property and sell up. I'm not staying.

> GARY *hoists up the section of timber framing for one wall. By whatever makeshift means, he holds that frame in place on the footings until he gets the adjoining frame section into position. He's then able to bolt the two sections together. It's an awkward job to be done single-handed.* DAVE *doesn't offer to help.* DAVE *squints to run his eye over the flooring.*

Sure that floor is level, mate?

GARY: Aww, shit... is it off?

> GARY *panics, grabs for his level to check the flooring. The silence is suddenly broken by the shrill, grating roar of a chainsaw. Then the sound stops just as suddenly.*

DAVE: What was that?

> DAVE *spots* SUE-ANNE *offstage first. He backs away, ready to bolt.*

Hey... uh—Gary...

> GARY *turns to look in the direction* DAVE *is pointing.*

GARY: Jesus, Sue-Anne—

> SUE-ANNE *comes belting towards* GARY, *armed with a small chainsaw.*

DAVE: Watch it, mate, I think she's—

> SUE-ANNE *switches on the saw again, flourishing it at* GARY.

SUE-ANNE: I've had a gutful! I mean it, Gary!

DAVE *is horrified to see* GARY *approach* SUE-ANNE, *however gingerly.*

GARY: Settle down, Sue-Anne. Settle down, babe.

SUE-ANNE: Shut up! I'm not listening to you!

DAVE *winces as* SUE-ANNE *stabs the chainsaw in* GARY*'s direction.* GARY *gets closer to take the saw from her.* SUE-ANNE *pulls away.* DAVE *is mesmerised by their strange dance.*

Come near me and I'll slice you up! I mean it!

GARY: Put it down, babe. Come on, you'll hurt yourself.

SUE-ANNE: I'm telling ya, Gary, I've had a gutful!

GARY: Let's talk about it, babe. Put down the saw.

SUE-ANNE: No way! No other way you'll listen to me, you mad bastard!

GARY: Come on, babe. Come on. I'm scared you're gonna hurt yourself.

GARY *steps forward and disarms her, switches off the chainsaw.* SUE-ANNE *instantly crumples, the fiery temper gone. She flops against* GARY *and sobs as* GARY *shooshes her, rubbing her back like a parent with a distraught child.* SUE-ANNE *is 19, scrawny, twitchy, brittle bleached hair. She's wearing a tight lycra halter top and leggings which are getting too small for her seven-month pregnant belly.*

SUE-ANNE: You say 'It'll be all right, Sue-Anne'. I hate this shithole of a place.

GARY: Sssh, come on, honey. You got me all worried before. I couldn't find you or the car keys.

SUE-ANNE: Had a gutful. Drove into town.

GARY: That's no good. You don't want to do too much driving.

SUE-ANNE: I hate this place.

GARY: Sshh, come on… It'll be all right, Sue-Anne. We'll be right.

SUE-ANNE: I dunno, Gary…

DAVE *hovers at a distance, feeling like he's intruding on a private moment.* SUE-ANNE *suddenly regains her spirit and stabs her foot into the chainsaw.*

Anyway, there's your bloody chainsaw.

GARY: Thanks, babe. Get a good deal from that bloke?

SUE-ANNE: In the end. Whingey little bugger.

GARY *laughs and pulls her close.*

GARY: That's my girl.

DAVE *grins, relieved to see the mood improved.* SUE-ANNE *suddenly pays attention to him, spinning to face him, waspish.*

SUE-ANNE: Whatchou gawking at, mate? Think we're mad as cut snakes, do ya?

DAVE: No madder than a lot of people I've met.

SUE-ANNE: You were scared, werencha?

DAVE: You didn't aim it at me.

SUE-ANNE *suddenly barks a laugh, friendly, drawing* DAVE *in on it.*

SUE-ANNE: Bullshit! Your eyes were out on stalks!

DAVE: [*laughing*] Maybe a bit.

SUE-ANNE: [*to* GARY] Who is he?

GARY: From the burned-down place.

SUE-ANNE *goes closer to him, bouncing from toe to toe.*

SUE-ANNE: Yeah? You own the place? You gonna live there?

DAVE: No. I'm just

SUE-ANNE: Be great to have neighbours living there.

DAVE: Sorry, can't help you. I won't be hanging 'round for long.

SUE-ANNE *suddenly lunges towards him and pushes her face right in front of him.*

SUE-ANNE: How old d'you reckon I look?

DAVE: Oh…

SUE-ANNE: Look older than nineteen, don't I? That's because Gary's got us living out here like derros. I'll end looking about thirty by the time—

GARY: We are not living like derros.

SUE-ANNE: Yeah, yeah, all right. My skin's already gone all—

GARY: Say it's not true, Sue-Anne.

SUE-ANNE: [*irritated by* GARY*'s interruption*] What? What do you want me to say?

GARY: Tell him it's not true what you said. We are not living like derros.

SUE-ANNE: Yeah, cool it, Gary. He knows I'm just crapping on.

GARY: Say it.

SUE-ANNE: What?!

GARY: I want to hear you say it.

> SUE-ANNE *speaks like a polite little girl.*

SUE-ANNE: We are not living like derros.

GARY: Thank you very much.

> SUE-ANNE *pulls a face to* DAVE *about what a pain* GARY *is.* GARY *keeps on working doggedly.*

SUE-ANNE: Forgot what I was saying now. Thanks a lot, shithead.

> GARY *is acutely aware of* DAVE *watching the two of them.*

GARY: You're thinking how come I'm so much older than her, aren't you?

> GARY*'s ready for an argument, but* DAVE *returns him a laid-back smile.*

DAVE: I'm not thinking anything.

> SUE-ANNE *dances over to* DAVE.

SUE-ANNE: Guess how we met.

DAVE: Well, I don't—

SUE-ANNE: He was sent to spy on me. But he fell in love with me instead.

DAVE: Yeah?

> *Even* GARY *loosens up. When he talks about meeting* SUE-ANNE*, there's obvious pride and devotion in his voice. They tell the story in tag-team style, like a familiar routine.*

GARY: I was working for a bloke when I first got back to Sydney. Doing compo investigations for him—

SUE-ANNE: Pretty scumbag job, eh? Following people around taking photos of them putting out their garbage and that.

GARY: Scumbag is right. I hated it.

SUE-ANNE: I did my back in.

GARY: She was working at Coles New World.

SUE-ANNE: What a shithouse job that was.

GARY: Sue-Anne had a fall at work—

SUE-ANNE: Some moron spilt caramel topping everywhere.

GARY: Wrecked her back.

SUE-ANNE: It's still chronic. Might be in a wheelchair by the time I'm thirty.

GARY: Anyway, I was the stupid mug who had to spy on her. Catch her out for faking.

SUE-ANNE: Which I wasn't.

GARY: Which she wasn't.

SUE-ANNE: I could see him out the front window of the house. Sitting in his little van. The most pissweak spy.

She laughs affectionately. GARY *grins back, adoring.*

GARY: Anyway—on the second or third day—

SUE-ANNE: The second day.

GARY: Sue-Anne come over and poked her head in the van. Nearly jumped out of my skin.

SUE-ANNE: He was asleep. Head rolled back, mouth open, little bit of dribble right here—

She barks a laugh.

GARY: Get out of it. I just had my eyes closed. Sue-Anne goes 'G'day'.

SUE-ANNE: I'm just a friendly sort of a person.

DAVE: I can tell.

GARY: We got talking. One thing led to another.

SUE-ANNE *points with exaggerated gestures at her pregnant belly.*

Aww, Sue-Anne, don't make it sound like that.

SUE-ANNE: What?

GARY: Tell him we really love each other.

SUE-ANNE: [*mock dutifully*] We really love each other.

GARY: Oh, Sue-Anne…

SUE-ANNE *can tell that* GARY *is really hurt now. She dives across to cuddle him and changes tack—heavily sincere now with* DAVE.

SUE-ANNE: Gary loves me to death. Even before we found out I was pregnant, Gary said he was gonna look after me—no matter what happened with the compo case.

> GARY *and* SUE-ANNE *kiss, intimately enough to make* DAVE *uncomfortable.* SUE-ANNE *breaks the kiss suddenly and breathlessly goes on with the story.*

Anyway, I didn't even know I was pregnant. I thought I had a tummy wog, y'know. I was gonna get rid of it, but Gary chucked a mental and by the time he finished, it was too late.

> GARY *tries to sounds confident, but it comes out sounding like a plea for reassurance.*

GARY: By the end, you were glad you didn't have the abortion, werencha babe?

SUE-ANNE: Yeah, yeah. So, anyway, that's how come I ended up with this old geezer, banged up, camping out in the middle of fucking nowhere.

DAVE: When's the baby due?

GARY: March 18.

SUE-ANNE: Gary's building a house for me and the baby with his own bare hands. Romantic, hunh?

DAVE: Most romantic thing I've heard all day.

SUE-ANNE: [*bristling*] You taking the piss, mate?

DAVE: Not at all.

GARY: Yeah, well, all this yackety-yack—the baby'll be in high school before the house is finished.

> *He makes a big show of returning to his work.* DAVE *doesn't shift from his comfy spot.* SUE-ANNE *scampers over to sit beside* DAVE.

SUE-ANNE: Guess how we got this land.

DAVE: Bought it with the compo money.

SUE-ANNE: You're joking. That compo money'll probably take years to come through. Bloody lawyers. Guess again.

DAVE: [*laughing*] I don't know. You'll have to tell me.

SUE-ANNE: Gary inherited it! Don't you reckon that's incredible?

DAVE: Oh, well, lots of people inherit land or money—

SUE-ANNE: Yeah, but Gary never had a proper family! He lived in foster homes and that—

> GARY *is working doggedly, but he's aware of* SUE-ANNE*'s chatter.*

GARY: Stop blabbing, Sue-Anne.

SUE-ANNE: Gary's mother died when he was a kid and his dad just dumped him.

GARY: I can hear ya, Sue-Anne. Stop bullshitting.

SUE-ANNE: And then just when I got banged up, Gary gets a letter from a lawyer saying his father snuffed it and left him this land. Maybe he felt guilty about dumping Gary and that's how come he died just at the right time to give us a place to live—

GARY: This house'll never get finished if you don't switch off your mouth, Sue-Anne.

DAVE: I can't see you finishing this place by March.

SUE-ANNE: That's what I tell him. I reckon we should sell it and—

GARY: [*starting to lose his temper*] That's enough.

> SUE-ANNE *grabs the Indian cloth bag and rummages through the chocolate bar wrappers.*

SUE-ANNE: I'm starving.

GARY: Have a sandwich.

SUE-ANNE: I don't want a sandwich.

GARY: Have a cheese sandwich.

SUE-ANNE: I don't want a fucking cheese sandwich.

GARY: Have a cheese sandwich. You haven't had one serve of calcium today—

SUE-ANNE: [*grinning to* DAVE] He's got this pregnancy book he reads. Nags me till I go mental.

GARY: Excuse me if I want our baby to be healthy.

SUE-ANNE: Babies get born okay when their mothers are smack addicts or starving in the desert or that.

GARY: Yeah, well, I never heard of a baby born when its mother lived on Violet Crumble bars.

SUE-ANNE: Hey, maybe we should call it Violet if it's a girl.

> SUE-ANNE *triumphantly fishes out a Violet Crumble bar and takes a huge bite out of it, taunting* GARY.

GARY: I'm not joking, Sue-Anne. You're gonna eat some decent food.

> SUE-ANNE *'s mood suddenly switches back into shrill waspish mode.*

SUE-ANNE: It's my body, right? I didn't even want this fucking baby. You tricked me into it.

GARY: Don't say stuff you don't mean, Sue-Anne.

DAVE *starts backing away, feeling the tempers heat up again.*

DAVE: I'll—uh—see you guys later.

SUE-ANNE: Every day I think—I wish I had the abortion.

GARY *winces when she says it.*

GARY: Please, Sue-Anne. You know that's not true.

SUE-ANNE: I'm nine-fucking-teen. Why would I want to get stuck with a baby living in a tin shed?

GARY: It's not a tin shed. It'll be a bloody good house.

SUE-ANNE: Hey, mate, don't you reckon—?

She turns to appeal to DAVE. *It's only then she realises he's gone.*

SUE-ANNE: Where'd he go?

GARY: Snuck off. Couldn't stand to hear you squawking and swearing and going off your brain as usual.

SUE-ANNE *dances over to throw an arm around* GARY, *laughing.*

SUE-ANNE: He thought we were a pair of galahs. A pair of desperates.

She grabs GARY *in a hug. He laughs and gives in to her boisterous affection.*

SCENE TWO

Between scenes, parts of the house will appear, marking the progress in the building. GARY *puts up more sections of the frame.*

The house site is in darkness. GARY *and* SUE-ANNE *enter from the campsite.* GARY *is carrying a portable gas lamp.*

GARY: Watch where you're going. Aww jeez, shouldn't be wearing those shoes.

SUE-ANNE: Quit nagging me.

GARY holds up the gas lamp for her to see the work in progress.

Oh Gary! It's starting to look like a real house!

GARY smiles proudly, then hoists the gas lamp through into the 'house'.

GARY: Door goes right here. Let me carry you across the threshold.

SUE-ANNE: No, you'll hurt my back.

GARY: Come on.

He hoists her up in his arms and she giggles as he carries her through the opening in the frame where the front door will be. We see them moving around 'inside' the house.

SUE-ANNE: Put me down. I feel like a big whale.

GARY puts her down and uses the gas lamp to show her the floor plan of the house.

GARY: This is the lounge/dining.

SUE-ANNE: Is it big enough?

GARY: Houses always look small at this stage. It's deceptive. Kitchen in here.

SUE-ANNE: Kitchen? What do you use one of those for?

GARY: Don't panic. I'll cook. Watch your step. Lot of offcuts there, babe. Our room. Be a window right here. We'll see down into the valley sitting up in bed.

SUE-ANNE: Oh yeah… that's gonna be gorgeous.

GARY: And then next door, it's the baby's room.

SUE-ANNE: Oh, look at it. It's gonna be so sweet.

GARY: Plenty of room for a cot down that end, and a proper bed when it's bigger.

SUE-ANNE: And we'll need a cupboard or something, for its little tiny clothes and stuff.

GARY: I'm gonna build a change table that comes down from the wall on a hinge—like this.

He demonstrates on the imaginary wall.

SUE-ANNE: What's a change table for?

GARY: [*laughing*] You're not funny, Sue-Anne.

He steps out of the house and guides SUE-ANNE *carefully over the edge.*

Soon—and I'm not promising when—I'll put a verandah on 'round here. So there's plenty of shade for the little bloke to play.

SUE-ANNE *suddenly stops and gasps.*

You okay?

He holds her close, belly to belly.

SUE-ANNE: Feel that?
GARY: What?
SUE-ANNE: Just keep your hand there. That!
GARY: Oh yeah! Is that a foot?
SUE-ANNE: I think so.

GARY *is overwhelmed, dropping his head against her, full of emotion.*

GARY: Oh, Sue-Anne. I love you, babe.

With their arms around each other, GARY *holds the gas lamp up to light their way back to the campsite.*

SCENE THREE

The house site. Daytime. The frame of the house is now in place, with the skeleton of walls, windows and doors forming. GARY *is sawing timber with a handsaw and hammering together roof trusses.* DAVE *is strolling around the site, checking out the progress.*

GARY: Roof tin'll be delivered when she's thirty-six weeks. Lockup by thirty-eight weeks. That gives me two weeks to do me best with the hot water and a bit of a kitchen before the baby comes.
DAVE: Cutting it pretty fine.
GARY: We'll get there. Even if I have to work all night.

He pumps his sawing arm with extra force, revved up by the urgency of his words.

DAVE: [*laughing*] You're a mad bastard, Gary.

GARY *jerks upright.*

GARY: Beg yours?

DAVE: I mean you might actually get it built, seeing as you're such a mad bastard.

He punctuates this with a killer smile. GARY*'s determined not to be charmed.* DAVE *squints to look carefully at the join* GARY *is hammering.*

Phoo… sure that's square?

GARY: Oh—bugger it—I thought it was.

He scrambles to check the angle with a set square.

DAVE: Probably just the angle where I'm sitting.

GARY *glares at* DAVE, *irritated.*

GARY: You done anything about selling your place?

DAVE: Oh yes. I should push them along a bit. I'm getting sick of living in the garage.

GARY: The house worth saving?

DAVE: Burnt right through the frame. The old bloke had the kerosene heater on—

GARY: Your dad?

DAVE: Yeah. Looks like he had a heart attack and knocked the kero heater when he fell over.

GARY: He never got out?

DAVE: Might've already been dead from the heart attack.

GARY: I'm sorry, mate.

DAVE *answers calmly, explanatory rather than emotional.*

DAVE: He was a miserable old bloke. It was a miserable house.

GARY: [*blurting out*] Jesus, you're a cold bugger. [*Embarrassed by the disgust evident in his voice*] Sorry, mate. Sorry, if that sounded—

DAVE: No worries.

GARY: Wrong things come out my mouth sometimes and—I can never hide how I'm feeling.

DAVE: Yeah, I know. Your feelings are so close to the surface, I can almost see them through your skin.

GARY: Anyway, it's your family. None of my business.

DAVE: Family doesn't worry me either way.

GARY: What—was he some kind of arsehole, your dad?

DAVE: I wouldn't say that. No one in that house made each other very happy. Nothing out of the ordinary. Looked to me like I'd do less damage all 'round if I stayed away.

GARY: I was always deadset to kill my father.

> *Despite his effort to sound light-hearted,* GARY*'s high-octane anger rushes through his body.*

When I was ten years old, I marched into the Tae Kwon Do school and I said 'Teach me how to kill a person'. They all pissed themselves laughing.

DAVE: I'm not surprised.

GARY: I'd've killed him. I would've done it.

DAVE: I believe you, mate.

GARY: The bastard died before I had a chance to kill him.

> *He throws his body into sawing timber.* DAVE *watches him carefully, then spots* SUE-ANNE *driving up the road.*

DAVE: Here she comes.

> GARY*'s face breaks into a smile.*

GARY: Not a delicate little flower, is she, eh?

> SUE-ANNE, *now thirty-four or thirty-five weeks pregnant, runs clumsily up towards the house.*

How'd it go?

SUE-ANNE: Dave! I'm glad you're here! You were gonna tell me some story about a cop.

GARY: What did the doc say?

> SUE-ANNE *is busy with her own agenda.*

SUE-ANNE: [*to* GARY] Did you know he used to live in Casablanca? And America and Thailand and Italy and—

GARY: Did the doc give you the okay?

SUE-ANNE: [*addressing* DAVE, *irritated by* GARY*'s voice in her ear*] I really envy you, mate. I'll never go anywhere.

GARY: I'll take you overseas. Once we get set up here, we'll get some money together.

SUE-ANNE: Pig's arse. [*Making a great show of plonking herself down beside* DAVE.] At least I get to hear about interesting places when you're here.

GARY: Stop showing off, Sue-Anne.

SUE-ANNE: [*laughing, to* DAVE] Sounds like my father, doncha reckon?

GARY: You're not impressing him. She's not impressing you, is she, Dave?

DAVE *shrugs and smiles, wanting to stay out of it.*

SUE-ANNE: Gary's old enough to be my father. Easily.

GARY: Tell me what the doc said.

SUE-ANNE *swings around and barks it at him.*

SUE-ANNE: Everything's fine. So don't go on at me.

GARY: What position is the baby lying in? Were your blood tests all—

SUE-ANNE: If you're so interested, why don't you go to the fucking doctor and let him poke around inside you!

GARY *stops, sucking in some deep breaths.*

GARY: If you want to rile me up, Sue-Anne, you're wasting your breath.

He returns to work. SUE-ANNE *is sulky, wanting attention.*

SUE-ANNE: Hey Dave. Wanna stay for dinner?

GARY: What?

SUE-ANNE: [*to* DAVE] He thinks you're a bludger.

DAVE: I know.

SUE-ANNE: But I want you to stay for dinner, anyway.

GARY: [*warning*] Sue-Anne. What's this in aid of?

DAVE: Forget it. I can look after myself.

SUE-ANNE *suddenly shouts with teary indignation.*

SUE-ANNE: What's so weird about me wanting some company?

GARY: Okay, babe. Stay for dinner, Dave.

DAVE: Oh, umm…

SUE-ANNE: I'll go crazy up here without people to talk to!

GARY: I said he can stay.

But SUE-ANNE *is in full flight, ignoring the fact that* GARY*'s given in.*

SUE-ANNE: We can't have a baby in a dump like this—

GARY: Come on, honey. Dave's staying for dinner.

SUE-ANNE: We should let somebody adopt it—

GARY: Sue-Anne—

SUE-ANNE: Give it to people who can give it a proper life.

GARY: Don't say that, Sue-Anne.

SUE-ANNE: I'm just saying—

GARY: Take it back.

SUE-ANNE: What?

GARY: Don't you ever say that. Take it back. Take it back.

> SUE-ANNE *freezes, frightened by the tone in his voice. He holds her with a challenging look. Then* SUE-ANNE *crumples into sobs.*

SUE-ANNE: My back's killing me, Gary. I don't mean to be such a bitch. It's my back.

> GARY *encircles her in his arms.* SUE-ANNE *flops against him limply, sobbing. He rubs her back tenderly.*

GARY: Ssshh. Come on. Poor baby.

SUE-ANNE: It just hurts all the time now. Now the baby's so heavy.

GARY: [*to* DAVE] She can't take the painkillers, because of the baby.

> DAVE *nods, keeping well away.*

Sssh, come on, babe. Have a lie down and I'll give you a back rub after tea. You might as well stay for dinner, Dave.

DAVE: Oh—uh—

GARY: Stay.

SCENE FOUR

It's night. The only light is from the portable gas lamp. GARY, SUE-ANNE *and* DAVE *sit on the ground or perch on part of the house.* SUE-ANNE *is asleep, stretched out next to* GARY *with a sleeping bag draped over her. There's a pile of empty beer cans and* DAVE *and* GARY *are both drunk and maudlin.* GARY *is unconsciously attentive to* SUE-ANNE, *rearranging the covers, stroking her hair, etc. These are stories* GARY *has told many times before—probably in pubs, over many beers. He self-consciously sees himself as Gary-the-storyteller, as a colourful character shocking people with his hard-luck stories, nursing the pain of his background with self-dramatising, romantic care. But the real pain is there too.*

GARY: One day the old man sends me and my big sister off to stay with Nana. When I say 'Nana' you got a picture of some lovely old lady, right?

DAVE: Makes butterfly cakes, sings lullabys, smells of mothballs—

GARY: All that shit. Well, not this bitch. She didn't like kids and she was nasty with it, you know? Anyway, a week later, he drives us home again. Mum's not there. She'd been really sick and that, so I'm going 'Where's Mum?' and he wouldn't answer me. I'm seven years old, right? Seven years old.

DAVE: Yeah.

GARY: He never even told me she died. This friend of my mum comes over—nice lady—and she says 'Hop in the car, Gary. You're going to your new house today.' So I'm thinking, 'Whacko. New house. Dad'll be there. Sister'll be there.' Only it's strangers. Foster parents. Dickheads. Fair dinkum, I don't know how they pick out some of these people to look after kids. I was seven years old and one bloke belted me like he was killing a dog with a shovel. Made me eat my dinner on the back porch like a stray. I ended up biting that fuckwit on the leg. They moved me again.

DAVE: Jesus, mate. Someone must've been nice to you.

GARY: No, sure, I'll grant you that. The last foster parents—they were Salvos—they were nice. But by then Gary was a little shithead. Acting up. Ended up in juvenile detention. Four years.

DAVE: Four years! Shit…

GARY: Stayed out of trouble since then but.

DAVE: Moving around.

GARY: Prawn trawler. Oil rig. Abattoir. Sitting on bulldozers in the desert in WA. And all the time I was thinking 'If I ever find that bastard, I'll kill him.'

DAVE: Sounds like you've told that story a fair few times.

GARY *suddenly flares into anger.*

GARY: You got a problem with that?

DAVE: 'Course not. But I mean—

GARY *stands up groggily, spitting out the words.*

GARY: Hey. This is my life, mate. You eat my food and drink my beer and then you have a go at me. Well, fuck you.

Sophie Lee as Sue-Anne in the 1996 Playbox Theatre Centre / Q Theatre production. (Photo: Geoff Beatty)

Shane Connor as Gary in the 1996 Playbox Theatre Centre / Q Theatre production. (Photo: Geoff Beatty)

DAVE: Okay, Gary—I wasn't—

GARY: This isn't some story. This is my life.

DAVE: I know. But telling the story doesn't seem to do you a lot of good.

> GARY's *fierce stance—ready for a fight with* DAVE—*suddenly turns in on himself. He presses his bunched fists against his own chest.*

GARY: I know that. I know that. I've got this anger in me. I can feel it in me. That's why I've gotta build this house. Understand what I'm saying, Dave?

DAVE: Yeah, I reckon I—

> GARY *is on a roll, gabbling, desperate for* DAVE *to understand.*

GARY: I know Sue-Anne can seem like a little bitch. People've treated her like dirt. She's got reason to be a bitch. But we look after each other—

DAVE: I can see that.

GARY: Building this house, Sue-Anne and the baby. This is my last chance. I know that.

> DAVE *nods.* GARY *makes an effort to settle himself down.*

DAVE: I'm sorry, Gary. Didn't mean to offend you.

GARY: No, no, I'm sorry, mate. I've gotta concentrate on getting on with people. When you don't live in a proper family—with everyone being nice to each other—it's hard—you know—I'm not explaining this very well…

DAVE: No, I get you.

GARY: I watch other people—with their friends and their kids and that—and I copy how they talk to each other. I'm trying to learn how to be a person who isn't fucked up. But I fuck it up a lot. Someone says something to me and I get it wrong and—y'know…

DAVE: Yeah, it's like learning a foreign language.

GARY: Beg yours?

DAVE: You can learn all the right words and get by, but every now and then you miss some little idiom and you end up saying something stupid or rude.

GARY: [*shrugging*] Anyway… I'm sorry. I'm just doing me best.

DAVE: I know you think I'm a cold bugger.

GARY: No, mate, I don't.

DAVE: No, no, I realise what I must look like to you. But thing is, it's not like—I mean, I see what's going on for other people. I do see things. I feel things. But—I don't want to make things worse for anyone.

GARY: So okay—you finish up your business here, then head off to nowhere in particular, right? How long can you keep going like that?

DAVE: Been getting away with it for quite a few years.

> GARY *shrugs and mutters something to himself.*

What?

GARY: It wouldn't be enough for me. That's all I'm saying. You don't look like—well, it's none of my business.

> DAVE *is nervous, as if* GARY *can see him acutely.*

You look like a bloke who doesn't know what the fuck to do next.

> *They sit, staring at the gas lamp, for a moment.*

Want another can?

DAVE: Nah… I better get home.

GARY: Yeah. Early start tomorrow.

> DAVE *gets to his feet and steadies himself, a bit drunk. He heads off.*

Are you okay to get home? Wanna borrow a torch?

DAVE: I'm okay.

> *He disappears into the darkness.*

SCENE FIVE

A country town motel room. CHRISTINE *is on the phone. She is in her late thirties but her hard surface and beaten look can make her seem older. She is dressed in serious business clothing, but on the slightly tarty side.* CHRISTINE *has made a point of keeping her speech rough, in defiant, chip-on-the-shoulder style. As she talks on the phone, she's in the process of tossing a briefcase down, removing her shoes, loosening her clothing and opening a bottle of wine. She has the same tightly-controlled energy and anger that* GARY *has—but in* CHRISTINE*'s case much more tightly controlled. It comes out in a hard, abrasive approach to the world. She's someone who expects to find battle and sees it even when it's not there. She's been disappointed so many times, she won't be such a mug ever again— even in the most mundane of encounters.*

CHRISTINE: No, I'm now staying at the Squatter's Rest Motor Inn. [*Pause.*] Yes, I did leave a message. [*Pause.*] I travel with my job. [*Pause.*] Is it too much to ask one of the solicitors to ring me back? [*Pause.*] Don't get a tone with me, missy. [*Slowly as if talking to a moron*] I explained to the other woman that my surname is different to the surname on the documents. [*Pause.*] No. Not a married name. I changed my name by deed poll. The point is—I need to know where I stand with this piece of property. [*Pause.*] I beg your pardon? Does your boss know you speak this rudely to clients? What's your name? [*Pause.*] I'd just like to know your name. Yes, I'm writing it down. [*Pause.*] Did someone from that legal firm draw up the will? [*Pause.*] Whoever drew up that piece-of-shit must've got his law degree out of a Cornflakes packet. [*Pause.*] I am not interested, honey. Just get someone to call me back.

> *She slams down the phone hard. She takes a deep breath to damp down the anger and then turns on a TV set. With the sounds of the TV burbling away, she drinks a large gulp of wine.*

SCENE SIX

The house site. Daytime. GARY *is building.* SUE-ANNE *bellows out from a distance.*

SUE-ANNE: Guess where I've been!

> GARY *keeps building.* SUE-ANNE *gallops over to him.*

Went and had a look at Dave's place.

GARY: Shouldn't've done that.

SUE-ANNE: Dave won't know. He's driving all the way to the travel
agent. Be gone all day.

GARY: I don't care, Sue-Anne. It's none of our business.

SUE-ANNE: Yeah yeah. Dave won't ever know I was even there.

GARY: It's sneaky.

> SUE-ANNE *sulks.*

SUE-ANNE: Won't tell you what I saw then.

GARY: Suit yourself.

> SUE-ANNE *scuffs away, petulant.* GARY *pointedly concentrates
> on work.* SUE-ANNE *lasts about three seconds.*

SUE-ANNE: Bet you really wanna know what his place is like.

> GARY *stops working, knowing she won't let it drop. But he's
> curious too. He looks at her—okay then. She perks up
> instantly.*

It's so creepy over there. Like, the house is all black and burnt-
up, but you can kind of tell the shape it used to be. Like a
skeleton. Garage is still there. That's where Dave's got himself
set up. He's got a bed and a stove and that. No windows but and
junk everywhere. A shithole. Why's he staying there?

GARY: He's gotta sort himself out a bit. That's why.

SUE-ANNE: No way I'd stay there. Place gives you the heeby-jeebs.
Did his dad die in the lounge room or the bedroom or—?

GARY: I don't know.

SUE-ANNE: Errgghh… couldn't help thinking about it. What's a
burned-up person look like?

> GARY *goes back to work.*

GARY: That's enough, Sue-Anne.

SUE-ANNE: Like a burnt sausage? Or—

GARY: I said that's enough.

SUE-ANNE: Everyone in town reckons Dave's a real weird bugger.

GARY: You don't wanna pay attention to people telling tales.

SUE-ANNE: Lady in the post office said he never wrote to his parents
or anything—

GARY: And I said we don't listen to the bullshit they go on with. I make my own mind up about people.

SUE-ANNE: Didn't say I believed it, did I?

GARY: Dave's not doing anyone any harm.

SUE-ANNE: Hey. Hey. I like Dave. I liked him first atchally.

GARY: Not doing anyone much good either, I s'pose.

> SUE-ANNE *is bored.*

SUE-ANNE: You nearly finished?

> GARY *indicates the house frame.*

GARY: What's it look like to you, Sue-Anne?

SUE-ANNE: I mean now. You nearly finished now.

> GARY *reluctantly downs tools.*

GARY: What?

SUE-ANNE: I'm hungry.

> GARY *sees the cheeky look on her face and can't help smiling back. He walks slowly towards her.*

GARY: Then why doncha just say 'Make us a sandwich, Gary'.

> SUE-ANNE *squeals as he scoops her up and carries her off.*

A cheese bloody sandwich.

SCENE SEVEN

A hardware store. VINCE *works behind the counter. He's about twenty-one, weedy, nervous, his face in a permanent flinch as if expecting to be yelled at. He slumps and shrinks his body back from people as if apologising for himself constantly. Most people terrify* VINCE, *so* CHRISTINE *reduces him to a speechless, quivering stupor. She is in her business clothes, brisk, wanting to get this business out of the way.*

CHRISTINE: Vince?

VINCE: Uh…

CHRISTINE: Are you Vince? Aren't you sure if you are?

VINCE: Uh, yeah. Vince.

CHRISTINE: Glad we've sorted that out. Bloke at the motel said go down the hardware store and Vince'll give you directions to Lot 102 on the Buckman's Creek road.

> VINCE *opens his mouth but can't get any words out.*

I won't bite, you know. Can you give me directions?

VINCE: I guess.

CHRISTINE: Well, he said you'd done some deliveries along that road.

> VINCE *nods.*

What kind of deliveries? Hardware?

VINCE: [*nodding*] And building materials… and that…

CHRISTINE: Well—what's going on? Deliveries to who?

VINCE: To the bloke building the house.

CHRISTINE: Someone's building a house?

VINCE: Bloke who owns the place.

CHRISTINE: Gary?

> VINCE *flinches at the sharp tone in* CHRISTINE*'s voice and nods nervously.*

Oh my God! He's building a house?

> VINCE *nods again, shrinking back behind the counter further.*

Ohh Jesus… bloody Gary… what's he… oh, that'd be right… What's he using for money?

VINCE: Sorry?

CHRISTINE: How's he paying for the stuff you deliver?

> VINCE *freezes with terror and* CHRISTINE *is intrigued.*

Your hands are shaking. Have you got some sort of problem?

> VINCE *shrugs. He just wants* CHRISTINE *to go away.*

Do you know what Gary thinks he's doing up there?

VINCE: Look, I dunno… I mostly talk to his girlfriend.

CHRISTINE: Oh, Christ! He's got a woman up there. He's dragged some poor bloody woman there.

> *She turns to see* VINCE *cowering behind the counter, shaking.*

Well, Vince—can you draw me a map? A map to find Lot 102?

The house site. Daytime. GARY *is on a ladder, hammering the roof structure together.* DAVE *and* SUE-ANNE *sit nearby. She's even more hugely pregnant.*

SUE-ANNE: Dave reckons you'd need twice this many paddocks to grow sheep on.

GARY: Does he?

DAVE: This is strictly hobby farm size.

GARY: You two sit there on your puddings all day, so you'd know all about sheep.

SUE-ANNE: [*to* DAVE] He's mad. For a start, where are we gonna get the money to buy the little sheep?

GARY: I can hear ya, Sue-Anne. And I've told you before—this winter, I'm gonna use the chainy to cut firewood, drive it to Sydney and sell it. Forty or fifty bucks a trailer load.

DAVE: Hard work, Gary. Knackering to get decent money that way.

GARY: For someone with a work allergy like you, mate, it would be.

DAVE: Sure you left enough room for the guttering there, mate?

GARY: [*a moment of panic*] What? [*Realising* DAVE *is teasing*] You come and do it then, smartarse.

SUE-ANNE: [*teasing, singsong*] Ooh, Gary's getting the shits.

> GARY *reaches across too far on the ladder and nearly loses his balance. The ladder wobbles.* GARY *whoops with fright.*

Want me to hold it steady?

GARY: No way. I don't want you doing physical stuff.

> *He starts to come down the ladder and it wobbles dangerously again. Reluctantly,* DAVE *gets up and goes over to hold the ladder steady.* GARY *and* SUE-ANNE *roar and whistle with mock amazement.*

I don't believe it!

SUE-ANNE: Hey, Gary, we were wrong! He can walk!

GARY: Don't do yourself a damage, mate!

DAVE *smiles happily.*

DAVE: I won't.

GARY *gets down the ladder and confronts* DAVE *seriously.*

GARY: Listen, Dave… I've been—uh—I've been thinking about it. Speed things up a lot if you work with me—

DAVE: Come on, mate, you know—

GARY: Hold on. Let me finish. What I'm saying is, you help me get this place up. Then I help you rebuild the old house. Work together.

DAVE: Oh. Ohh… look… thanks, Gary—

GARY *looks firmly at* DAVE—*this is a serious offer.*

GARY: It could be a good partnership.

DAVE: Thanks for the offer. Really, mate. But I've been talking to this bloke. He's lined me up some work in Spain. I get an apartment, have a bit of a holiday before the summer season starts.

GARY: Well, you know, if you'd rather—

SUE-ANNE: Oh, der, Gary. Like he'd rather stay in this shithole instead of going to Spain.

GARY *notices* SUE-ANNE *rummaging in her pocket.*

GARY: Hey, what's in your pocket?

He lunges across and pulls a handful of Violet Crumble bar wrappers out of her pocket.

Jesus H. Christ, Sue-Anne. This baby'll be born with rotten teeth.

SUE-ANNE: That's stupid. They don't even have teeth when they come out.

GARY: You eaten anything decent today?

SUE-ANNE: Yeah.

GARY: Like hell.

He stalks off towards the campsite. SUE-ANNE *bellows after him.*

SUE-ANNE: It's my body, shithead! [*Turning to* DAVE, *grinning*] I reckon if God exists, he sent Gary to me.

DAVE: Pardon?

SUE-ANNE: He really loves me—don't you reckon?

DAVE: Uh… yeah. I do.

SUE-ANNE: Every guy I was ever with treated me like shit, except Gary.

> GARY *marches back up to them, carrying a cardboard box full of fruit and vegetables.*

GARY: I did not buy these to make the tent look beautiful.

> SUE-ANNE *pulls a face.*

DAVE: Mmm, those peaches look all right.

SUE-ANNE: You eat it then.

GARY: For Christ sake, this bludger'll eat his way through all of it, if you don't.

> DAVE *bites into a peach, dribbling it down his chin.*

DAVE: Very tasty.

> GARY *grabs a bunch of grapes and starts stuffing them in his mouth.*

GARY: Look at these. They're beautiful.

SUE-ANNE: [*laughing*] I'm glad you guys are happy.

> GARY *and* DAVE *make a great show of enjoying the fruit.* GARY *grabs* SUE-ANNE *and tries to entice her to eat grapes. She giggles and they wrestle affectionately.*

DAVE: Car turning in the gate.

> SUE-ANNE *and* GARY *follow* DAVE*'s eyeline to watch the approaching car.*

SUE-ANNE: Know who that is?

> DAVE *and* SUE-ANNE *are too interested in the arrival to notice that* GARY*'s smile has faded, his face set hard.* SUE-ANNE *gallops clumsily down towards* CHRISTINE *as she walks towards the house site.*

Hi.

> GARY *nods in greeting to* CHRISTINE.

Who's she?

GARY: My sister.

SUE-ANNE: Yeah!? Really?

CHRISTINE: How are you, Gary?

GARY: All right.

CHRISTINE *registers* SUE-ANNE*'s pregnant belly.*

CHRISTINE: Oh my God, you poor little bitch.

SUE-ANNE: Whatchou say? What she say, Gary?

CHRISTINE: [*to* GARY] You're building a house.

SUE-ANNE: Oh, der—she's a genius, your sister.

> CHRISTINE *ignores* SUE-ANNE*, dancing around her. She just wants to get this sorted out and get out of there.*

CHRISTINE: Were you told this piece of land was a joint bequest?

> GARY *nods.*

SUE-ANNE: Joint bequest? What's that mean?

> *She looks to* GARY*, but he's too rigid with tension to answer.*

Gary? Hey! Answer me.

CHRISTINE: It means this land was left to more than one person.

SUE-ANNE: What other person? You?

GARY: Shut up, Sue-Anne.

CHRISTINE: I'm the other beneficiary.

SUE-ANNE: Beneficiary?

CHRISTINE: I own half.

SUE-ANNE: What! Did you know that?

> GARY *doesn't answer.* CHRISTINE *starts to bristle, losing the reasonable tone.*

CHRISTINE: We have to sort this out, don't we?

SUE-ANNE: Is that really your sister?

GARY: I said be quiet, Sue-Anne.

CHRISTINE: What the hell made you think you could do this?

GARY: Why don't you piss off?

SUE-ANNE: Yeah. Piss off.

CHRISTINE: Listen to me, Gary—

SUE-ANNE: [*mimicking her*] 'Listen to me, Gary.'

CHRISTINE: I'll deal with this through the solicitor.

> *She spins on her heel and heads back to her car.*

SUE-ANNE: How come you never told me—?

GARY: Shut up, Sue-Anne.

> *He has a sudden change of heart—his mood lurching into something much more open and vulnerable.*

Christine! Hold on a minute! Christine?

> CHRISTINE *stops and turns back.*

Look, I know I should've—I don't wanna make trouble with you but—I know I should've…

> *She stands there, not wanting to meet the needy, sentimental gaze* GARY *is sending her.*

How are ya, anyway? You look good.

CHRISTINE: I'm all right, Gary.

GARY: Looking flash. Still working for the same mob?

CHRISTINE: No. New job. I'm on the road most of the time now.

GARY: Oh yeah? Selling?

CHRISTINE: No.

GARY: What kind of work then?

CHRISTINE: Auditing work really.

SUE-ANNE: What's auditing mean?

GARY: Christine went to tech. Did accounting and that.

SUE-ANNE: I don't give a stuff. I wanna know what auditing means.

CHRISTINE: I'm working for a company with various retail chains. I go 'round to the branch stores to check the books and so on.

SUE-ANNE: Make sure people haven't got their hands in the till.

CHRISTINE: Among other things.

SUE-ANNE: A nark job.

GARY: Shut up, Sue-Anne.

SUE-ANNE: [*guffawing*] I bet everyone hates your guts when you roll into town.

> GARY *suddenly moves closer to* CHRISTINE *with a gush of emotion. She backs off, stiffens.*

GARY: All we've got is each other, Christine.

SUE-ANNE: What about me?

GARY: Let's do this together, Chrissie.

CHRISTINE: Do what? Some pathetic idea you've got about living—

SUE-ANNE: Hey! Don't I get a say in this, shithead? How come you—

> DAVE *reaches out a hand to restrain* SUE-ANNE *gently.*

DAVE: Let them talk for a minute.

> CHRISTINE *flashes her attention onto* DAVE.

CHRISTINE: And who are you? Are you part of this ridiculous setup?

> DAVE *turns on a charming smile.* CHRISTINE *doesn't respond, stony-faced.*

DAVE: I'm not part of any set-up.

GARY: Look—Chrissie—all we've got is each other.

CHRISTINE: What does that mean? If we've only got each other then we're well and truly rooted, aren't we?

GARY: Remember when I ran away that time and I found where you were living?

> CHRISTINE *is determined not to get drawn into the painful memories* GARY *is revving up. But despite herself, she gets upset, squashing it down with bad temper.*

CHRISTINE: I am not interested in—

GARY: I can remember clear as anything. You had that blue check school uniform on. You must've been fourteen or fifteen—

CHRISTINE: I was twelve.

GARY: At least I came and looked for you.

SUE-ANNE: [*barracking for* GARY] Yeah. Right.

GARY: I always thought you'd track me down.

> GARY *turns to* SUE-ANNE *for a sympathetic audience.*

When I first got dumped at the foster home—I remember thinking 'My big sister'll come and rescue me'.

CHRISTINE: Your 'big sister' was nine years old.

GARY: We can help each other now.

CHRISTINE: No. No, I don't think so.

SUE-ANNE: Gary never said you were such a bitch. Ran out on him when he was a little kid—

CHRISTINE: [*to* GARY] Will you tell your little bit of scrag to shut her mouth?

GARY: Don't talk to Sue-Anne like that.

SUE-ANNE: He's just asking you to help him.

CHRISTINE: Listen, honey, I've helped him plenty. I don't know what bullshit he's spun you. But I've done a shitload of family duty. [*To* GARY] Forget to tell her how many times I've bailed you out of trouble, Gary? How much money you've sucked out of me?

GARY: I'm not asking for money, Chrissie.

SUE-ANNE: Shit, I see what you mean, Gary. What a bitch.

GARY: I never said that, Sue-Anne.

CHRISTINE: [*to* SUE-ANNE] He's a bottomless pit, sweetheart. You'd do better pissing off now.

SUE-ANNE: Get fucked. What would you know about—

Meanwhile, GARY *has sparked into a stiff-necked rage, stabbing his finger at* CHRISTINE.

GARY: Don't you tear me down. I'm not gonna let you tear me down.

CHRISTINE: This is a bloody balls-up, isn't it? Why did he make it a joint bequest? Typical of that bastard—leaves a mess behind him. Has a good go at wrecking things even when he's dead.

GARY *is circling, concentrating on not losing his temper.*

I want to sell my share of the land and you don't have the money to buy me out, do you?

GARY *shakes his head. The more he tries to settle down, the more* CHRISTINE*'s words wind him up.*

Then you can't build a house here, can you?

GARY. This is my house.

He walks to his tool box.

CHRISTINE: Be realistic for once in your bloody life, Gary. You cannot build a house on land you don't own. It's being sold. Simple.

GARY *keeps his back to her, facing the toolbox.*

GARY: I'm building this house. I'm not gonna let you tear me down.

DAVE: Come on, Gary—don't make it any worse.

CHRISTINE: Oh my God… you've really…

GARY *turns around with a gun in his hand.*

GARY: You better go.

SUE-ANNE: Fucking hell! I didn't know you had a gun.

DAVE: For Christ sake, put the gun away, mate.

GARY: I just want her to get away from my house.

CHRISTINE: You poor mad bastard…

GARY: Piss off. Now.

CHRISTINE *shakes her head and goes.* GARY *sucks in some deep breaths and forces his body into a controlled posture. He walks slowly back to the tool box and puts the gun back.* DAVE *and* SUE-ANNE *are both too scared of the gun to say anything. They hold their breath, watching to see what* GARY *will do next.* GARY *grabs tools and timber and hurls his body back into work.*

SCENE NINE

Between scenes GARY *works—putting on the roofing tin.*

A corner in a grubby, small town pub. CHRISTINE *sits by herself with a bottle of wine open on the table in front of her. When she sees* DAVE *come in, she's prickly and aggressive with him.*

CHRISTINE: Have you come here to talk me into giving Gary that land?

DAVE: Nup. Come in for a drink.

CHRISTINE *watches him carefully, standing by her table. She's still sharp and defensive.*

CHRISTINE: But while you're here, you're gonna have a go at me about—

DAVE *turns to her with a charming smile.*

DAVE: That's Gary's business. Nothing to do with me.

She doesn't take her eyes off him, noticing how he occupies the space with easy grace. When DAVE *turns back to address her again, she starts a little, feeling caught out for staring. He whispers to her, laughing conspiratorially as if they are already intimates.*

All the pub regulars are having a good stickybeak at you. Can't work you out.

CHRISTINE: Well, maybe you should really give them something to wonder about. Help me drink this wine.

DAVE: Yeah? Thanks. I'll get another glass from the bar.

CHRISTINE *watches him move across to fetch a wine glass and then slide himself into the chair. He knows she's watching him. She pours him a glassful.*

Thank you. Looks like my day's improving.

He flashes her a grin and she can't help smiling in reply. Then she fights the smile off her face—still wary of this guy.

CHRISTINE: You're a mate of Gary's.

DAVE: I'm the guy's next-door neighbour. That's about it.

DAVE *concentrates on enjoying his wine for a moment.* CHRISTINE *scrutinises him sharply, looking for accusation.*

CHRISTINE: But you think I'm a hard bitch.

DAVE: Eh? Look, I don't think anything. I'm just—

CHRISTINE: Gary's earbashed you about everything, I bet.

DAVE: I guess you could say that.

CHRISTINE: Has he done the big speech for you about when we were kids and all that?

DAVE: Yeah. It's quite a speech.

CHRISTINE: He wheels that out for anyone who'll listen, you know.

DAVE: Oh, I know.

CHRISTINE: He loves it. Making people feel sorry for him.

DAVE: Yeah. He has had a rough deal.

CHRISTINE: Lots of people get a rough deal.

DAVE: That's true too.

CHRISTINE: I could do a sob-story like that. Make you feel bloody sorry for me.

DAVE: I bet you could.

CHRISTINE: But I don't do it. Can't see the point.

DAVE: No. Fair enough.

CHRISTINE *fixes* DAVE *with a sharp look.*

CHRISTINE: Do you always agree with whoever's paying for the booze you're drinking?

DAVE *jerks his head as if she's socked him in the face, but he's laughing too.*

DAVE: Phew… Don't feel you have to hold back, Christine.

CHRISTINE: I'm in a shitty mood. Seeing Gary… seeing that little scrag of a girl—

DAVE: Sue-Anne.

> CHRISTINE *spits out the words, her whole body consumed with anger, much like* GARY.

CHRISTINE: And that poor baby. What chance has it got? Rule Number One—never have kids. If you're damaged—like me and Gary—the least you can do is not pass it on to some poor kid. Ohhh God… if I think about it too much, I'll get depressed.

DAVE: Yeah. Don't think about it.

> CHRISTINE *takes a deep breath. She realises she's just subjected* DAVE *to a mouthful.*

CHRISTINE: So how come I haven't scared you off?

DAVE: You're not angry with me, are you?

> *He grins at her and she finally lets herself smile back.*

CHRISTINE: So if you reckon you're not here to talk about Gary, what are you doing here?

DAVE: I've come to the pub for a drink.

CHRISTINE: But why are you having the drink with me?

DAVE: Look around…

> *He indicates the rest of the bar.* CHRISTINE *casts her eye over the other occupants.*

'Course I'd be sitting here, if I'm invited.

CHRISTINE: [*laughing*] God, what a line. Not even subtle.

DAVE: Maybe not subtle. But never bullshit.

CHRISTINE: Well, I feel like being flattered, so I will be.

> DAVE *settles into his chair, really relaxed now, sure where the evening is going.* CHRISTINE *looks around the bar.*

A lot of walking wounded 'round here, eh? You don't look like a local.

DAVE: I grew up here. Left when I was seventeen, but these mad bastards never leave. Why do you think I don't live here?

CHRISTINE: There are losers everywhere you go.

DAVE: That's why I don't stay anywhere very long.

CHRISTINE: To avoid things that might depress you, you roam the country.

DAVE *pays her the point for getting him right, but corrects the detail.*

DAVE: Roam the world.

CHRISTINE: I would've thought my poor, mad little brother and his scrag was one of the more depressing sights to be seen in the Southern Hemisphere.

DAVE: Yes and no. Something about Gary's—It demands your attention. [*Picking up the almost empty wine bottle*] Reckon we could get through another bottle of this?

CHRISTINE: Well, I'm going to need to drink a bit more before I can proposition a man I met three hours ago.

DAVE: Jesus, you're direct, aren't you?

CHRISTINE: Have I scared you off now?

DAVE: Not at all.

CHRISTINE: I'm staying in one of the cabins out the back. They can put it on my bill.

> *He fills their glasses with the last of the wine. She watches him carefully.*

You're another stray too.

DAVE: I don't like that word.

CHRISTINE: I mean we're both strays.

DAVE: I prefer to see myself as a conscientious objector in the world of relationships. Strays sounds too negative.

CHRISTINE: It is negative. It's a disability.

DAVE: I like my life.

> CHRISTINE *leans back and makes a show of scrutinising him.*

CHRISTINE: I've met guys like you.

DAVE: [*laughing*] Oh yeah?

CHRISTINE: Slippery.

DAVE: I don't bullshit anyone. I've got a few rules I stick to. Never promise anything I'm—

> CHRISTINE *waves her hand to stop him. She's smiling, even if she's saying critical things. And* DAVE *takes it from her because he can tell she likes him.*

CHRISTINE: Yeah yeah yeah—I'm very familiar with that speech. I've met guys like you before, remember.

DAVE: [*mock indignantly*] I want to be a unique individual, okay?

CHRISTINE: In fact, I used to fall for guys like you. Wham—Christine gets pulverised again.

DAVE: But not anymore.

CHRISTINE: No. I don't expect anything from anyone and I'm not disappointed. You're completely safe.

> *She tosses her room key across and he catches it. She laughs, relaxes a little.*

Maybe I should give Gary my share of that land and be done with it. Gary thinks he can—oh… Gary thinks too much.

DAVE: And you don't?

CHRISTINE: When I'm working, I don't let myself think about anything else.

DAVE: But what about when you finish work?

CHRISTINE: Well… I'm usually in a motel room somewhere. And I've worked out the formula—exactly the right amount of alcohol plus a certain kind of TV show and you can stop thinking. And if it doesn't work and I start getting sorry for myself—then a nice stray fuck solves that one.

> *She looks around to see a look of distaste on* DAVE*'s face.*

Think that's disgusting, do you?

DAVE: Hey, I don't judge.

> *He feels the relaxed, benign mood darken as* CHRISTINE*'s body stiffens with anger again.*

CHRISTINE: Yes, you do. Guys like you say 'I don't judge'. But you fucking do. You watch people and you judge them.

> DAVE *starts to retreat from her.*

DAVE: Listen… ummm…

> CHRISTINE *can feel that he's shrinking away.*

CHRISTINE: Now I have scared you off.

DAVE: I told you—I've got a few rules.

CHRISTINE: Come on, I don't believe a guy like you's got a rule against exploiting a situation like this.

DAVE: No, I guess not. But I've got a rule about keeping clear of sad shit. Stuff that—

CHRISTINE: Stuff that makes you depressed.

DAVE: Yeah. So—

He hands her the room key. She doesn't reach to take it.

CHRISTINE: Stay.

DAVE: No. Look, Christine—

CHRISTINE: You won't have to see me again. I mean, I won't be coming back to this wretched place, I can promise you.

DAVE: I know.

CHRISTINE: We'll never lay eyes on each other again.

But he holds the key out to her—he's not going to be persuaded. She tries a cheeky smile.

You don't have to worry about wounding my dignity. I don't have any.

She barks a laugh and DAVE can't help a smile. But he's still firm. She tries straight and needy appeal.

Stay with me. Look, mate, I just—Please stay.

She can see he won't change his mind. Finally she takes the key from his hand and he disappears into the darkness. She stays slumped against the bar stools.

SCENE TEN

The house site. It's dark, but GARY is still working by lamplight. SUE-ANNE is prowling around him. She is grimly thoughtful rather than hysterical.

SUE-ANNE: We've had it now. You've fucked it now.

GARY: We'll be okay.

SUE-ANNE: She'll go to the cops and then we—

GARY: She won't go to cops.

SUE-ANNE: Well, lawyers then!

GARY: I'll work it out.

SUE-ANNE: Ya reckon? How come you never said someone else owned this place—

GARY: Half. We own half.

SUE-ANNE *starts to cry, limp and feeble.*

SUE-ANNE: Where are we gonna live? Where's this little baby gonna live?

GARY: Here. In this house.

SUE-ANNE *looks at him and shakes her head.*

SUE-ANNE: Oh Gary…

GARY: Don't cry, babe.

SUE-ANNE: You said she won't change her mind. So we're stuffed.

GARY *runs over to hug her.*

GARY: Please don't cry, honey. I'll talk to her. I'll fix it.

SUE-ANNE *pulls away, shaking her head.*

SUE-ANNE: I can't listen to you anymore. Have to do this before I change my mind.

GARY: Getting yourself all jazzed up about nothing, babe.

SUE-ANNE: I'm leaving.

GARY: Don't talk rubbish, Sue-Anne.

SUE-ANNE: Going back to Sydney. Get this baby adopted.

The instant he hears the word 'adopted', GARY stops working. He's gulping for air as if she's winded him.

GARY: Don't say that, Sue-Anne. Not even joking. Not even trying to rile me up. Don't you ever say it.

SUE-ANNE: This baby'll be better off with a proper family and that. I've thought about it—

GARY: Take it back. Take it back. You can't say it.

SUE-ANNE *rushes around, collecting up her belongings.*

SUE-ANNE: I'm gonna do this before you change my mind.

GARY: Sue-Anne—

He chases after her, frantic. SUE-ANNE is panting, partly from exertion and partly because she's revving herself up to go through with it. When GARY sees the bag, his panic increases.

You're not really going, are ya Sue-Anne? Say you're not going.

The pain in his voice almost gets to her. But she just chants loudly, keeping up her frantic packing.

SUE-ANNE: I'm not listening to you. I'm not listening to you.

GARY: You're tearing out my heart, Sue-Anne.

SUE-ANNE: I'm taking the ute. I'll leave it in town for ya.

> GARY*'s crying now, his voice breaking as he pleads with her.*

GARY: Don't do this, babe.

> *He blocks her path down to the ute. She stands her ground, but head down to avoid meeting his eyes.*

SUE-ANNE: Let me get past.

GARY: Don't leave. Don't give our baby away. I can't let you do it.

SUE-ANNE: Let me go, Gary.

> *She is suddenly frightened of him, as he blocks her path.*

You're not gonna hurt me, are ya?

GARY: Ohh, Sue-Anne… I'd never hurt ya. I'd never do that…

> *The suggestion that he might've hurt her seems to kill the last energy to resist that* GARY *has. His body slumps and* SUE-ANNE *takes the chance to scoot past him.*

Don't go, Sue-Anne. Stay. Stay.

> *She disappears offstage.* GARY *is heaving for breath as he watches her go, winding himself up into a fit of frustrated rage. He circles, but the fight's gone out of him. He's more torn up than angry now. He prowls the site, the life knocked of him. A torch beam picks up his face as someone approaches. He looks up and sees that it's* DAVE.

DAVE: I saw Sue-Anne go past in the ute.

GARY: She's gone.

DAVE: Gone?

GARY: Left me. She's going to get the baby adopted. That's what she said.

DAVE: Sue-Anne says a lot of things. Probably just having a tantrum. She'll be back. She'll—

GARY: No. No. She meant it. I know her. She'll do it. She'll do it.

> DAVE *watches* GARY *circling, wheezing for breath.* DAVE *is torn between his urge to back right away, avoid this, and his immediate concern for* GARY.

DAVE: Look, I reckon in the morning, she'll be in a better mood and you can—

GARY: No! I said no! This is it. She's gone. She's gonna do this thing. I know her.

> DAVE *is nervous of* GARY's *potential violence. He takes another step back.*

DAVE: All right, mate, all right. Look, do you want me to stick around for a while?

GARY: You don't have to.

DAVE: I'll stay around if you reckon—

GARY: I'll sort myself out.

DAVE: Get some sleep, mate. In the morning, I'll come over—we can work out what to do. She might even be back by then—

> GARY *shakes his head emphatically.*

Well, anyway, I'll be back—first thing. We'll talk, eh mate? Sure you'll be okay tonight?

> GARY *turns to face the house and flicks his head—it's not really a nod, but* DAVE *chooses to take it as assent.*

Okay then. See you in the morning. Get some sleep.

> DAVE *disappears into the darkness and at first* GARY *doesn't realise he's gone.*

GARY: She's torn out my heart, Dave. I can feel it. I can feel it. She's torn out my heart.

> GARY *turns around to see that* DAVE *hasn't heard him. He's gone.* GARY *goes over to the toolbox and takes out the gun. He sits down in the frame of the front doorway of the house. He sits for a moment, working himself up to do it. Then he swings the gun around with the barrel in his mouth.*

END OF ACT ONE

ACT TWO

SCENE ONE

The house looks deserted, abandoned. Eventually, DAVE *walks up towards the house. He hears a noise from inside and freezes. He shouts out with the false confidence of a person who's very rattled.*

DAVE: Someone in there?

> *There's the thump of someone dropping something heavily and then* CHRISTINE *appears in the front doorway of the house.*

Jesus, you gave me a fright.

CHRISTINE: If it's any consolation you gave me one.

> *An awkward silence.* DAVE *tries to sound relaxed and friendly in a detached way.* CHRISTINE *bungs on a bit of extra coolness and dignity to handle this.*

Thought you had your ticket booked.

DAVE: The cops needed me to hang around. Make a statement. I found the body.

CHRISTINE: Yes, I heard.

> *Another awkward silence.*

DAVE: You back here to—uh—

CHRISTINE: To get this place sold.

DAVE: [*attempting humour*] You'll flood the market.

CHRISTINE: [*icily*] Well, I'm sorry.

DAVE: Hey. Hey, just kidding. [*He can't stand the silence.*] Well, I'll get out of your way.

> *He starts to wander back down. Meanwhile,* CHRISTINE *has noticed someone turning in the gate.*

That's Gary's ute.

They watch the ute pull up.

CHRISTINE: Oh my God… Does she even know?

DAVE: Sue-Anne! Need a hand?

> *But he doesn't actually make any effort to go and help.* SUE-ANNE *struggles the last way up to the house site, pushing a rickety second-hand pram.*

SUE-ANNE: [*to* CHRISTINE] What the fuck are you doing here?

CHRISTINE: I'm just here to see about—

SUE-ANNE: You've got a hide turning up here after what you've done.

> CHRISTINE *doesn't attempt to argue or defend herself.* DAVE *tries to keep the mood jolly by leaning down to inspect the baby in the pram.*

DAVE: Boy or girl?

SUE-ANNE: Boy.

DAVE: You had him—?

SUE-ANNE: Two weeks ago. Just after the cops told me.

> DAVE *nods sympathetically. When he sees that* SUE-ANNE *has turned her sights back on* CHRISTINE, *he quickly jumps in again.*

DAVE: The cops said you were putting the baby up for adoption.

SUE-ANNE: That's what I told them then, yeah.

CHRISTINE: But you've decided to keep him.

> SUE-ANNE *spins for a shrill attack on* CHRISTINE.

SUE-ANNE: Are you saying I can't look after him?

CHRISTINE: No—

SUE-ANNE: You saying I'm not good enough to look after my own kid? Are ya?

DAVE: Hey… she's not saying anything, okay, Sue-Anne.

SUE-ANNE: [*to* CHRISTINE] I don't wanna hear another word out of your filthy mouth, okay? You come here and you wreck everything—I dunno why—maybe you just can't help being a poisonous bitch. You wouldn't even listen to Gary and now he's dead. And it's your fault. It's your fault.

CHRISTINE *remains passive, eyes down.* SUE-ANNE *has exhausted herself for the moment.* DAVE *deftly wheels her around to look at the baby again.*

DAVE: He's a cute little gremlin. What's his name?

SUE-ANNE: Clint.

DAVE: G'day, Clint.

SUE-ANNE *finally lets herself smile and be gooey about the baby.*

SUE-ANNE: Watch out, Clint—this guy's a prize bludger and bullshit artist.

DAVE: Don't believe a word she says, little bloke.

SUE-ANNE: Wake him up and I'll tear out your throat.

DAVE *retreats from the pram with mock terror.*

DAVE: You… uh… back to have a look at the place?

SUE-ANNE: Nuh. Me and Clint are gonna live here.

CHRISTINE: Eh?

SUE-ANNE: I've got a right to stay here.

CHRISTINE: But you can't seriously—

SUE-ANNE: Don't you tell me what I can't do.

CHRISTINE *doesn't dare speak, but she throws an anxious look to* DAVE—*do something, this girl is crazy.*

DAVE: The house isn't finished, mate.

SUE-ANNE: I'm gonna finish it.

CHRISTINE: What!

SUE-ANNE: You saying I can't do it? Are ya?

DAVE: No one's having a go at you. But there's a lot of work before this place is—

CHRISTINE: That's right.

SUE-ANNE: If you never come and poured shit on Gary, he'd be here to look after me and Clint.

DAVE: Okay, settle down, Sue-Anne—

CHRISTINE: You're going to live—by yourself with a two-week-old baby—in a half-finished house in the middle of nowhere?

SUE-ANNE*'s pumped-up bravado and anger suddenly crumple into tears.*

SUE-ANNE: Where else am I supposed to go? I dunno what to do...
I'm so tired... I'm so fucking tired all the time...

> *She stumbles and knocks the pram.* DAVE *reaches out to grab the handle and stop the pram careering away.* CHRISTINE *suddenly finds herself comforting the weeping* SUE-ANNE *against her chest.*

My back hurts all the time... it's worse when you don't sleep, you know...

> *She is hiccuping with tears.* CHRISTINE *is awkward with her, physically—not used to being a nurturing person. She stiffly puts her arm around* SUE-ANNE.

CHRISTINE: Ssshh. It's okay. It must be hard.

SUE-ANNE: Fucking oath it's hard. I couldn't feed him. I tried doing it. It hurts. How do people ever do it? I dunno... The nurses in the hospital, they kept saying 'Come on, Sue-Anne, just do this and that', as if it's so bloody easy. I'd like to see those bitches do it. This one freckly witch of a nurse—she kept barging in to my room and hissing at me about getting him adopted... as if I couldn't look after him... but I want him with me... I can't give him away...

CHRISTINE: I understand that. 'Course you want him.

SUE-ANNE: But I don't know anything about babies... what you're meant to do with them and that...

> CHRISTINE *shepherds* SUE-ANNE *over to sit somewhere.* CHRISTINE *is uncomfortable—saying what she thinks someone ought to say in this situation.*

CHRISTINE: Look, it must be difficult to manage on your own. How about I drive you back to Sydney? You can... um... stay at my place... until you get set up.

> SUE-ANNE *isn't really listening. She's just sniffling against* CHRISTINE*'s shoulder.*

SUE-ANNE: It's my back. It hurts all the time.

CHRISTINE: I'll take you to a doctor as soon as we get back to Sydney.

> SUE-ANNE *rallies as suddenly as she collapsed, shaking free from* CHRISTINE.

SUE-ANNE: Nuh. I'm not going back. Me and Clint are staying here.

CHRISTINE: Come on, Sue-Anne, I don't think that's a very good idea.

> SUE-ANNE *is still teary, but her tone is urgent and determined.*

SUE-ANNE: This is Gary's house. He wanted us to live here, all together.

> CHRISTINE *throws a look of appeal to* DAVE.

DAVE: It'll be winter in a couple of months, Sue-Anne. They get snow up here. This house isn't even clad.

SUE-ANNE: I'll fix it up. We've got the tent and that for now. Me and Clint are staying here. I don't care what any of youse say.

CHRISTINE: [*to* DAVE] Would it cost much to get this place clad?

DAVE: D'you mean make it livable or finish it?

CHRISTINE: If I paid a local builder, could they get it livable by winter?

DAVE: Yeah, a decent builder'd have no worries.

CHRISTINE: That's what we'll do, Sue-Anne. I'll get someone to fix the place up for you.

> CHRISTINE *and* DAVE *then realise that* SUE-ANNE *has fallen asleep, her head on* CHRISTINE*'s lap.* CHRISTINE *feels awkward to find herself in this position. She looks up to see* DAVE *staring at her, puzzled.*

What are you staring at?

DAVE: Nothing. I mean, I'm just—

CHRISTINE: Can't believe this—is that it?

DAVE: Well… yeah.

CHRISTINE: I'm not a complete monster, you know.

DAVE: I know.

> CHRISTINE *doesn't want any sort of intimacy with* DAVE. *She makes her voice hard and cold.*

CHRISTINE: Anyway, I'm sure she won't really want to stay very long.

DAVE: No. She'll change her mind pretty quick.

CHRISTINE: She's upset now. Got this idea in her head.

DAVE: Yeah.

CHRISTINE: Might be worth spending a bit of money on this place. Get a better price for the land, wouldn't I?

DAVE: Most likely, yeah.

There's a squawk from the baby in the pram. DAVE *and* CHRISTINE *both look frightened of the alien creature inside.*

CHRISTINE: Would it be hungry or something?

DAVE: Jesus, I dunno. I don't know anything about babies.

CHRISTINE: Neither do I.

The baby squawks again.

[*Indicating* SUE-ANNE] Should we wake her up?

DAVE: Don't think she's got much more idea about babies than we have.

There's no more sound from the pram.

CHRISTINE: Have a look at it. Check it's okay.

DAVE *gingerly steps over to peek in the pram.*

DAVE: Back asleep.

CHRISTINE: Thank Christ.

DAVE *laughs.*

What?

DAVE: You're a poor little bugger, Clint. Stuck here with three of the most incompetent, ignorant people on the face of the earth.

CHRISTINE *can't help responding with a smile, but she turns away and fights the urge to smile.*

CHRISTINE: You don't have to hang around. We can manage here.

DAVE: Oh… rightio.

He sidles off.

SCENE TWO

VINCE *makes his way up towards the house site. He's extremely nervous—he's not looking forward to this.*

VINCE: Hello. [*His hello is so quiet that he clears his throat and has another go.*] Hello. Anyone around?

When CHRISTINE *appears,* VINCE *starts with fright.* CHRISTINE *is brisk—she wants to sort this out and get out of the place.*

CHRISTINE: Got everything on the list?

VINCE: Well—yeah… but—

CHRISTINE: Unload the truck by that stack of timber.

> VINCE *opens and closes his mouth gormlessly.*

Is there a problem? I can help you until the builder gets here.

VINCE: Oh no… I can unload no worries… but, um…

CHRISTINE: What?

> DAVE *strolls over.* VINCE *turns to grin at him, relieved to put off the moment of truth.*

VINCE: Oh. Dave.

DAVE: G'day, Vince. How are ya, mate?

> VINCE *smiles and shrugs.* CHRISTINE *is even more irritated to see* DAVE *here.*

CHRISTINE: Is there something you want?

DAVE: Saw the hardware truck drive past. Thought I'd come and say g'day to Vince.

CHRISTINE: I see. Well, you've done that now.

> DAVE *sits himself down, unfussed by* CHRISTINE*'s hostility.*

Comfortable?

DAVE: Yeah. Actually, I could handle a beer without too much difficulty.

> VINCE *guffaws and* CHRISTINE *flashes him a withering look.* VINCE *duly withers.*

[*Referring to the truckload*] Who's doing the job for you?

CHRISTINE: Doug Skinner.

> DAVE *stifles the urge to laugh and* VINCE *splutters into laughter.*

We spoke on the phone. He gave me a very reasonable quote.

> DAVE *laughs again, provoking* VINCE *into a guffaw.*

CHRISTINE: Look, I know there are two Dougs around here.

DAVE: Old Doug and Young Doug.

CHRISTINE: Yes and I'm employing Young Doug.

Ailsa Piper (left) as
Christine and Sophie
Lee as Sue-Anne in
the 1996 Playbox
Theatre Centre / Q
Theatre production.
(Photo: Geoff Beatty)

Terence Crawford as
Dave and Ailsa Piper as
Christine in the 1996
Playbox Theatre Centre
/ Q Theatre production.
(Photo: Geoff Beatty)

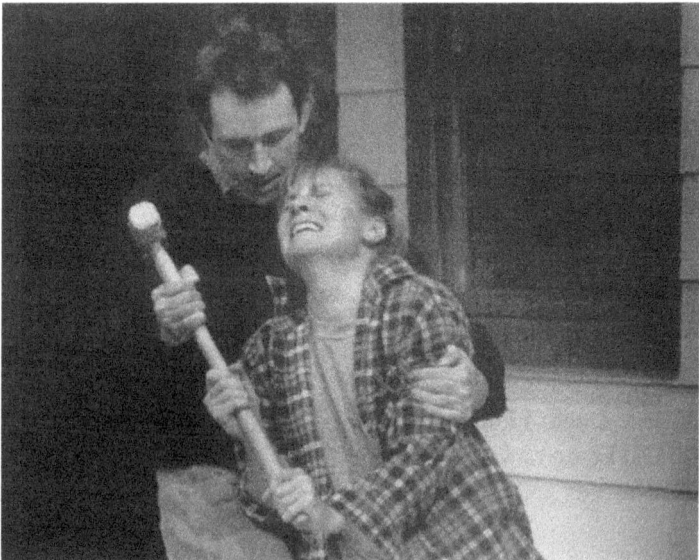

DAVE: Young Doug must be at least sixty-five. He's got arthritis, Parkinsons, and his brain's fried by a few too many swigs of pesticide.

CHRISTINE: Why is he called Young Doug?

DAVE: You should see Old Doug.

> VINCE *collapses with laughter again and he and* DAVE *enjoy the shared joke, much to* CHRISTINE*'s annoyance.*

CHRISTINE: Are you having a go at me?

DAVE: Doug Skinner's always been Young Doug. I guess he was young once.

> CHRISTINE *sighs, realising she's lost this one.*

CHRISTINE: I can find another builder. [*To* VINCE] Let's unload the truck.

> VINCE *hesitates, too scared of* CHRISTINE *to cross her.*

What is your problem? For Christ sake, spit it out.

VINCE: Not s'posed to unload the truck until you... um... pay for it.

CHRISTINE: Well, of course. COD. That's the arrangement I made with Mr Savasi.

VINCE: No, um...

CHRISTINE: What? What?

> CHRISTINE *is scaring* VINCE *so much, he can't answer.*

DAVE: What's the story, Vince?

VINCE: Well... umm... before—before the bloke died—they had a lot of stuff on credit—

CHRISTINE: You mean Gary?

VINCE: Well, Sue-Anne used to sign for it. I'd load the ute for her.

CHRISTINE: Yes, okay, I understand the basics of commerce. There's a bit of money owing, is there?

VINCE: If it isn't paid off today, I can't unload the truck.

> CHRISTINE *wields her cheque book fiercely.*

CHRISTINE: Okay okay okay. I want to see a full list of the items on credit.

> VINCE *pulls out a handful of invoices stapled together.*

How much are we talking about?

VINCE: [*wincing, not wanting to say it*] I never really added it all up till today.

CHRISTINE: How much?

VINCE: Nine thousand four hundred and thirty-eight dollars twenty-seven.

> CHRISTINE*'s face falls and* DAVE *sucks in his breath in an 'ouch' gesture.*

Plus the three and half thousand for this lot. Sorry.

CHRISTINE: Why would you give someone like Gary that much credit?

DAVE: I can't imagine Joe letting anyone run up a tab.

VINCE: Uncle Joe never knew about it. I kinda fixed the invoices and stock records.

> CHRISTINE *goes over the invoices, trying to absorb her disappointment in being businesslike.*

DAVE: Joe'd eat you on toast for doing that.

> VINCE *flinches—it was a close call.*

VINCE: Well… y'know… she used to come in to the yard…

DAVE: And you thought that baby wasn't going to wait around.

VINCE: Wasn't her fault they were in a mess. She said they'd pay it back.

CHRISTINE: Well, Gary's not going to pay it back now, is he?

> *She finishes scribbling out a cheque and hands it to* VINCE. *He flinches as if the cheque is red hot.*

VINCE: Ta. Sorry.

CHRISTINE: Now can you unload the truck?

VINCE: No problem.

> *He escapes to the truck.* DAVE *can see that* CHRISTINE *is shaken.*

DAVE: It's a lot of money.

CHRISTINE: Cleaned out my savings actually.

DAVE: Oh, Christine… I'm sorry.

> *His sympathy is so straightforward and warm that it rattles* CHRISTINE. *She bristles, not wanting his sympathy.*

CHRISTINE: Well, it's certainly not your problem.

DAVE: Look, you've got the materials you need to get the job—

CHRISTINE: But no money to pay a builder now.

> SUE-ANNE *enters, tousled from sleep.* CHRISTINE *and* DAVE *watch her wander up.*

I just wanted to have this done—efficiently—then get out of here. [*To* SUE-ANNE] Feeling better?

SUE-ANNE: A bit.

CHRISTINE: Is he still asleep? Did you put the mozzie net over him?

SUE-ANNE: [*irritable*] Yes, I put the net over him.

> VINCE *comes past with an armload of building materials. He instantly goes shy and gormless when he sees* SUE-ANNE.

Oh, hi Vince.

VINCE: Hi.

> *He stands there for a moment, swaying under the awkward load he's carrying, staring at her with helpless devotion.*

SUE-ANNE: Yeah? What?

VINCE: Sorry about the money and everything. My uncle went ballistic.

> *He slopes off with the materials.*

SUE-ANNE: What's he talking about?

CHRISTINE: As usual Gary dropped shit and ran. Nine thousand bucks worth of cement and radiata pine this time.

SUE-ANNE: I'm sick of you badmouthing Gary. He built this fucking house, didn't he?

CHRISTINE: Most of it not fucking paid for.

SUE-ANNE: He never knew about that.

CHRISTINE: About what?

SUE-ANNE: How me and Vince worked out a deal.

DAVE: What—Vince gave you stuff and you didn't pay for it—that was the 'deal'.

SUE-ANNE: More or less, yeah.

CHRISTINE: Where did Gary think the materials were coming from?

SUE-ANNE: [*shrugging*] Out of the bank money.

DAVE: But that ran out.

SUE-ANNE: [*nodding and rolling her eyes about* GARY] Ages ago.

CHRISTINE: Well, the welfare account is dry. You might as well drive back to Sydney with me straight away.

SUE-ANNE: What! Why?

CHRISTINE: In fact—Vince! Put all of that back on the truck.

SUE-ANNE: You said you'd fix it up for me and Clint! I thought we'd have a house at least. Oh shit… what are we gonna do now…

> VINCE *staggers past with the same armload of materials. He sees* SUE-ANNE *is hopping around, upset, almost sobbing. He stops and stares at her, concerned. His staring irritates her.*

What?

VINCE: You okay?

SUE-ANNE: No! No, I'm not okay!

> CHRISTINE *flicks her head to* VINCE *to finish loading the truck. Reluctantly, he leaves.*

CHRISTINE: Look, Sue-Anne, there's no money for a builder. Maybe in a few months time, I can scrape together—

SUE-ANNE: You said—you said—didn't she say it, Dave?

DAVE: Well, yeah, but things aren't exactly—

> SUE-ANNE *'s anger starts to dissolve into tears.*

SUE-ANNE: Gary would've looked after us. Now there's no one to look after us. I can't build it myself, can I? How can I build a house with my fucked-up back and a little baby? Tell me what I'm supposed to do…

CHRISTINE: Ssh, Sue-Anne, for God's sake, shut up a minute. Let me think a minute.

> SUE-ANNE *wanders away, sobbing.* CHRISTINE *circles, frustrated, trying to think. Then she notices* DAVE *standing there.*

You could offer to help her. You could pick up some of this stuff and make yourself useful, couldn't you?

DAVE: Look, I'm not a builder.

CHRISTINE: Neither was Gary.

DAVE: Anyway, you know I'm—

CHRISTINE: Leaving soon. So you keep saying. [*She spins to seize on* VINCE *as a target.*] Why do you keep walking all the way around like that?

VINCE: Oh…

CHRISTINE: Go straight across the front.

> VINCE *freezes, glancing in terror from the doorway and back to* CHRISTINE *glaring at him.*

Why do you keep doing that?

DAVE: It's okay, Vince.

VINCE: Well… isn't that where he did it…?

CHRISTINE: What?

DAVE: That's right, mate.

> CHRISTINE *catches on and it knocks the wind out of her for a moment.* DAVE *tries to sound rational about it, but we can see that he's shaken.*

VINCE: Cops were saying it's always a real mess… when a person blows their brains out.

> DAVE *shrugs and nods.*

You found him, didn't you.

DAVE: Yeah.

VINCE: Was it…?

DAVE: A terrible thing to see—yeah, mate.

> VINCE *glances nervously at the front doorway, as if some ghoulish sight is about to loom up at him.*

VINCE: I didn't even want to come up here… gives me the creeps… y'know.

> DAVE *nods, aware that* CHRISTINE *is watching him. He avoids making eye contact with her.* VINCE *takes the load back to the truck.*

CHRISTINE: Maybe I could have a go at fixing up the house.

DAVE: Eh?

CHRISTINE: It can't be that hard to nail up a few bits of weatherboard, can it?

DAVE: Well, yes and no.

> *This plan is forming in* CHRISTINE*'s mind as she speaks. She tries to sound as confident as she can, to convince herself as much as the others.*

CHRISTINE: I can take two months leave from work. I'm sure I can work out how to do this stuff.

>SUE-ANNE *is still sobbing nearby.*

Stop blubbering, Sue-Anne. I'll fix up the wretched house.

>CHRISTINE *notices the amazed look* DAVE *is giving her.*

What's that look?

DAVE: Nothing. I mean—

CHRISTINE: It's a smirk. Why is it so ridiculous? I'm an intelligent capable person.

DAVE: You are.

CHRISTINE: I'm not a cripple. If I do my homework—take it slowly—I can do it.

>DAVE *shrugs and makes a 'go for it' gesture.* VINCE *goes past with another armload of materials.*

Vince. Change of plans. Unload that stuff again please.

>VINCE *throws a look of confused appeal to* DAVE *and* DAVE *makes a 'don't ask me' gesture.* CHRISTINE *notices that* VINCE *is mooning after the sobbing* SUE-ANNE, *hesitating.*

She's all right. I'll help unload.

>*The baby is heard crying offstage.* SUE-ANNE *looks up and groans—not again.*

I'll go.

>CHRISTINE *strides offstage towards the baby.*

SCENE THREE

Between scenes, loads of building materials and tools appear on the site.

The area looks like an active building site again. DAVE *is sitting there with a small pile of books, flicking through them with some amusement. Suddenly a small hunk of timber comes flying out a window of the house, narrowly missing* DAVE. *Then from inside, he can hear the sound of* CHRISTINE *bellowing with frustration.*

CHRISTINE: You bastard! You bastard of a thing! Go in! Go in! You bastard!

> DAVE *listens calmly.*

No! Oh no! Fuck it!

> *Then another missile—this time a hammer—flies out the door and he has to dodge sideways to avoid being clobbered.*

DAVE: Oy!

> CHRISTINE*'s enraged face appears in the doorway.*

CHRISTINE: Sit there at your own risk, mate.

DAVE: Having problems?

CHRISTINE: Damn thing won't fit. I kept shaving bits off and now it's too bloody short.

> DAVE *holds out the books.*

DAVE: Turn to the books for guidance.

> CHRISTINE *grabs some tools and has a go at a carpentry job in front of him.*

[*Reading book titles*] *The Complete Owner-Builder Manual*— gotta be some answers in there. *Carpentry Made Easy.*

CHRISTINE: Well, easy's what it fucking isn't.

DAVE: You're right. Can't learn this stuff from books.

CHRISTINE: So wise and yet somehow so bloody lazy. You wouldn't get off your bum and help me, would you?

DAVE: You wouldn't let me help you, would you?

> *He flashes her a dazzling grin and she turns away so she won't fall for it.*

CHRISTINE: No.

> *She tries to concentrate on the job. She gets increasingly flustered.*

The problem is that everything Gary did in this house is arse-about. Didn't do anything the proper way—like the diagrams in there.

DAVE: Building's not like that. There are ways and ways.

> CHRISTINE *makes a show of scrutinising* DAVE *carefully.*

CHRISTINE: Don't you have a life? Who are you? I've been trying to work it out—he's supposed to be the Happy Wanderer but still, here he is—hanging around like a limp dick. And you know what I think?

DAVE *tries to keep it jokey, but he's rattled.*

DAVE: Uh—oh.

CHRISTINE: This routine you've been trading on—mooching 'round the world being professional good company. Ski instructor all the women want to flirt with. Few months crewing on a yacht. Mind some rich mate's house for the summer. People want you around. But you're getting too old for it. Might start to look pathetic in a few more years. I reckon you're worried.

DAVE: Is that what you reckon, is it?

CHRISTINE: I could be wrong.

DAVE: You could be.

CHRISTINE *is having another go at the job, making more of a mess the more flustered she gets.*

CHRISTINE: Or maybe you get your entertainment watching other people make an almighty mess of things. Come over here to watch me and have a good laugh, eh?

DAVE: Hey, I'm not laughing at you. I'm admiring your guts. Reminds me of Gary.

CHRISTINE*'s body stiffens.*

CHRISTINE: Oh, that's it, mate. You can piss off now. I am not interested in comments from the Philosopher Bum. The floorshow's over. Piss off.

DAVE *puts up his hands—I surrender—and starts to go. As soon as he moves away from the house,* CHRISTINE*'s angry energy crumples. She flops on the ground, overwhelmed, tossing a tool down with a loud clang. A moment later* DAVE *is back.*

DAVE: Umm… you okay?

CHRISTINE *is fighting the urge to cry.*

CHRISTINE: What?

DAVE: Well, I heard—Thought you might've hurt yourself.

CHRISTINE: No.

> DAVE *starts to go again, but then sees that* CHRISTINE *is just sitting there limply.*

DAVE: Christine? Sure you're okay?

CHRISTINE: I can't do this. I don't why I ever thought I could do this.

DAVE: Come on, Christine…

CHRISTINE: Oh please—a pep talk from you, I don't need. This whole thing was a mistake. I don't know what I'm doing.

DAVE: Well, for what it's worth—

CHRISTINE: Piss off. I don't want to start howling in front of you.

> DAVE *hovers there, not sure what he can say, but not wanting to leave her.*

Oh my God. You're hanging around here because you feel guilty about Gary. That's it, isn't it?

> DAVE *doesn't answer, just stares at the house.*

Well, you shouldn't. Gary was doomed. Always was.

DAVE: Maybe… maybe.

CHRISTINE: It's nothing to do with you.

DAVE: You know I came over here that night. I could've stayed with him.

CHRISTINE: Wouldn't've made any difference—

> DAVE *jumps in, unusually passionate—he's wrestling with these ideas, anxious to get it right.*

DAVE: No. No. I know people say that—that it was inevitable he'd top himself sometime. But timing matters. It does matter. He was screaming tired that night. Been working eighteen hours a day for weeks. His judgement was off. If I'd stayed with him till the morning—talked him through that night—it would've been different. He might've tracked her down. Or thought about it another way. Or—

> CHRISTINE *doesn't want to engage with what he is saying.*

CHRISTINE: Well, hanging around here being guilty doesn't do Gary any good now.

DAVE: No. I know that.

CHRISTINE: And it's giving me the right royal shits. So go away and feel guilty somewhere else.

DAVE *nods slowly and leaves.*

SCENE FOUR

Between scenes, CHRISTINE *puts up part of the cladding on the house.*

The house site. CHRISTINE *moves between a building task and a pile of books and scraps of paper she's using to work things out. She is dogged, determined.* SUE-ANNE *is hanging around with the baby in a pram.*

CHRISTINE: Did you ever see proper plans for this place?

SUE-ANNE: I dunno… nuh.

CHRISTINE: Well, did Gary ever talk to you about how he planned to—

SUE-ANNE: He'd crap on. I just go 'Sounds grouse, Gary'. Never listened but.

Seeing CHRISTINE *so absorbed in work,* SUE-ANNE *sulks.*

Might go into town. I'm bored.

CHRISTINE *bristles, ready to blast her.*

CHRISTINE: Bored, are you, Sue-Anne? My heart bleeds for you. [*She takes a breath and modulates her tone.*] You could give me a hand.

SUE-ANNE: Dunno how to do it.

CHRISTINE: Neither do I. I'm using books, making the effort.

SUE-ANNE: Yeah, but you're prob'ly not a total deadhead like me.

She barks a laugh but CHRISTINE *doesn't smile. When* CHRISTINE *goes back to work,* SUE-ANNE *pulls out a cigarette and lights it.* CHRISTINE *notices her exhale smoke directly over the baby's pram.*

CHRISTINE: What's that in your hand?

SUE-ANNE: Aww, der, is it a cigarette?

CHRISTINE *snatches the cigarette from her hand and stomps it into the dirt.*

Hey!

CHRISTINE: Did you smoke when you were pregnant?

SUE-ANNE: [*lighting up another cigarette*] Nuh. Never did. Only took it up a few weeks ago.

CHRISTINE: What?

SUE-ANNE: Lot of stress on you when you have a baby. Specially a single mother.

CHRISTINE: Do what you like to your own body. You never smoke around that baby!

The baby starts crying.

SUE-ANNE: Thanks a million. Getting woken up's prob'ly bad for his health too. Worse. I bet it is.

She is now rocking the pram back and forth quite violently, taking out her annoyance.

CHRISTINE: Do you want to send him flying out?

SUE-ANNE: We don't have to listen to her, Clint. She's a poisonous bitch.

CHRISTINE *calms herself and returns to work.* SUE-ANNE *spots* DAVE *approaching.*

Dave! How are ya? Oh God, been so boring up here without you coming 'round.

DAVE: Hi, Sue-Anne.

CHRISTINE *and* DAVE *exchange a nod in greeting.*

I wanted to let you know I've finally sold my place.

SUE-ANNE: What? Oh shit... does that mean you're pissing off?

DAVE: I'm booked to fly out on the fifteenth.

SUE-ANNE: Leaving me here with her. Thanks a lot. I'll go mental.

CHRISTINE: Definitely? I mean, you've got a definite buyer?

DAVE: Looks like it.

SUE-ANNE: Hey, hey, Dave—at least stay for dinner tonight. We'll cook you dinner.

CHRISTINE: No, we won't.

SUE-ANNE: Dave's my friend. I'm inviting him.

CHRISTINE: I said no, Sue-Anne.

SUE-ANNE: [*to* DAVE] Jeez, I thought I was a bitch. Did she go to bitch university or something?

DAVE: Thanks anyway, Sue-Anne. I'll—uh—

He indicates that he's going.

CHRISTINE: Look, there are a few things I wanted to ask you about.

DAVE: Sorry?

CHRISTINE: Apparently Gary never had drawn-up plans.

DAVE: Oh… no, only in his head.

CHRISTINE: But did he talk about what he had in mind?

DAVE: Yeah. He had timetables. Lists. Talking about it calmed him down.

CHRISTINE: So you'd have some idea about how he saw things fitting together.

DAVE *pulls a doubtful face.*

I'm just asking if you wouldn't mind dropping over a couple of times—before you go—so I can— (ask questions)

DAVE: To get my head bitten off. No thanks.

CHRISTINE: The odd free beer in exchange for information.

He makes a big show of being nonchalant as he strolls off.

DAVE: I guess I can help out before I leave.

He goes. CHRISTINE *makes a point of not noticing. But on the sly she glances up as* DAVE *leaves. Then she notices* SUE-ANNE *smoking near the baby.*

CHRISTINE: You just blew smoke right in that baby's face!

She takes the baby from SUE-ANNE.

I'll hold him until you finish that thing. Hurry up.

SUE-ANNE *makes a petulant performance of sucking on the cigarette.* CHRISTINE *moves away, cradling the baby, staring up at the half-finished house.*

[*Whispering*] How's it going, anyway, you poor little bugger? I guess you think this is normal—don't know any different.

She shifts the baby into a more comfortable position, tucked into her neck, and decides it feels nice. Checking to see that SUE-ANNE *isn't watching, she inhales deeply, smelling the baby's head.*

SCENE FIVE

The house site. Daytime. SUE-ANNE *is feeding the baby with a bottle and* DAVE *is relaxing with a beer and a newspaper. Meanwhile, from inside the house, we can half hear* CHRISTINE*'s running commentary as she works.*

CHRISTINE: I get it. I get it. Line it up with the noggin there… and it fits like—yes, yes. Fit for me—please, please, fit… I'll be gentle… please fit for me…

> SUE-ANNE *puts the baby into the pram. Then she and* DAVE *hear the sound of* CHRISTINE *whooping.*

Yes! Yes! Yes!

> CHRISTINE *bursts out of the house, dancing around with exaggerated joy and triumph.*

It fits!

DAVE: Well done.

CHRISTINE: I just slotted it in, bit of a nudge. Perfect.

DAVE: Knew you'd get there.

> CHRISTINE *paces around, bursting with pent-up energy, not knowing what to do with this much good feeling. She leans down to address the baby in his pram.*

CHRISTINE: It fits, little baby. The most perfect bit of gyprocking you've ever seen in your life. I am going to finish this house for you, my tiny friend. Oh my God!

SUE-ANNE: What?

CHRISTINE: He's smiling!

SUE-ANNE: [*mimicking* CHRISTINE] 'It's just wind, Sue-Anne. It's not a real smile.'

CHRISTINE: No, no, this is a real one. He's looking right at me and smiling.

> SUE-ANNE *dashes over to look in.*

CHRISTINE: Oh… he's stopped.

SUE-ANNE: Supposed to smile at their mothers first, aren't they?

> DAVE *heads off a possible sticky moment by jumping in.*

DAVE: Talk to him about gyprock. That seems to crack him up.

SUE-ANNE: Fuck off. I'm not gonna talk to a little baby about gyprock.

CHRISTINE: There you go!

> SUE-ANNE *and* CHRISTINE *stare into the pram at the smiling baby.*

SUE-ANNE: Oh, look at that! Oh, Clint! All his little gummy bits! Hello, Clint! Hello, beautiful!

> *She exchanges a look with* CHRISTINE—*all their ill feeling momentarily obliterated by the flush of joy from the first smile.*

You gotta see this, Dave. He's so gorgeous! Who's a gorgeous boy? Who's a major spunk?

> DAVE *stirs himself to look into the pram. The baby's smile is infectious*—DAVE *grins broadly.*

DAVE: Hey, mate. That's a top notch smile you've got there. Hey, little fella. If you think gyprock's exciting, wait till she tries her hand at plumbing.

> *She looks—expecting that he's making fun of her. But he's smiling and* CHRISTINE *chooses to smile back. He picks the baby up and walks around with him, rocking back and forth on his heels.* CHRISTINE *and* SUE-ANNE *stare at him in disbelief.* SUE-ANNE *bursts into raucous laughter.*

SUE-ANNE: Jeez, you're good at that, Dave.

> *He pulls a face, a bit embarrassed.*

Too bloody good, mate. Make us wonder where you learned how to do it. [*Conspiratorially to* CHRISTINE] Know what? I bet Dave's got little kids all over the world. Teeny tiny Daves—all different colours—

> CHRISTINE *nods and laughs.* DAVE *is uncomfortable, but he endures the teasing.*

DAVE: I know that's not true. I'm very careful.

SUE-ANNE: [*mimicking* DAVE] 'I'm very careful.' How would you know? A bloke never knows for sure.

> DAVE *flinches, embarrassed.*

Whoa! Dave's embarrassed. His face is going all red!

> SUE-ANNE *and* CHRISTINE *enjoy a laugh together at his expense.* SUE-ANNE *dances over and tickles at him.*

Aww come on, Dave. Only teasing ya. Aww, look at his sulky lip.

> DAVE *hands the baby resolutely back to* SUE-ANNE.

[*To the baby*] Hey, gorgeous—gonna come into town with me and show everyone your little gums?

CHRISTINE: You're going to take him?

> SUE-ANNE *nods, putting the baby back in the pram, fussing over him, pulling faces at him.*

Too hot for him in that ute now. Wait till it's cooler.

SUE-ANNE: And do what, while I wait around?

> *She heads off with the baby in the pram.*

CHRISTINE: Got the list?

SUE-ANNE: Yes, I've got the list.

CHRISTINE: Don't sweet-talk Vince. We pay for stuff.

SUE-ANNE: I know. I know.

CHRISTINE: Get the soy milk formula this time. The book said that rash on his face could be—

SUE-ANNE: Yeah yeah, I know what your book said. I'll get cow formula—

CHRISTINE: No, get the soy one!

> SUE-ANNE *rolls her eyes—she was deliberately riling* CHRISTINE *up.* SUE-ANNE *flounces offstage.* CHRISTINE *turns back to the house and hoists up another sheet of gyprock. She suddenly grins, the flush of satisfaction coming back.*

When it slotted in there— [*Shaking her head, lost for words*] A very tricky bit—one of Gary's dodgy angles—and I nailed the bugger. Can't tell you how good it feels.

DAVE: I can see. You look amazing. Lit up.

> CHRISTINE *laughs with child-like joy. She paces around, trying to absorb this unfamiliar feeling.*

CHRISTINE: Not used to this, I can tell you. Haven't felt this good since—Bit of a shock to the system. Haven't felt like this since... forgotten what this felt like.

SCENE SIX

Between scenes, the gyprock debris is cleared away and a bit more of the house is finished off.

The pub at night. DAVE *is at the bar, carrying a six-pack of beer and counting his change. He hears* SUE-ANNE *squawk from the other end of the bar. He is apprehensive as she rushes over to him, drunk and over-excited.*

SUE-ANNE: Dave!
DAVE: Had a bit to drink, Sue-Anne?
SUE-ANNE: Been in the Ladies' Lounge!

> *She squeals, finding the idea of the Ladies' Lounge very amusing.*

DAVE: I better drive you back.
SUE-ANNE: I got the ute.
DAVE: I'll drive you back.

> *She grabs onto him. He endures it.*

SUE-ANNE: You're such a nice guy, arencha Dave?

> *She is wobbly on her feet so* DAVE *gently leads her over to a chair. He tries to prise her hands off him but she clings on.* DAVE *gives in and sits in a chair next to her.*

Hey... You should hear the stories they tell about you around here.
DAVE: Oh yeah.
SUE-ANNE: About your Dad. What a dickhead you were. I don't believe them but. I go 'Bullshit. Dave's a top guy. A beautiful person.'

> *She pulls* DAVE *closer and tries to kiss him. He gently eases her away.*

DAVE: Whoa... come on, Sue-Anne.
SUE-ANNE: I'll come up and stay the night at your place. She's looking after Clint.

DAVE: Oh no... I don't really—

SUE-ANNE: You must be lonely up there all by yourself, Dave.

> *She has another try at a kissing him. He rebuffs her more firmly this time, but still gentle.*

DAVE: No, Sue-Anne. That's not going to happen.

> SUE-ANNE *is drunk and confused.*

SUE-ANNE: Well... well...

DAVE: What's this about all of a sudden?

> SUE-ANNE*'s buoyant drunken state dips into blackness.* DAVE *softens his tone.*

This isn't what you want. This won't fix anything, will it?

> *He holds her steady as she stands there swaying, utterly lost and desolate, for several moments. He feels a great rush of pity for her.*

Come on, Sue-Anne... Now—can I give you a lift home?

> *She shrugs limply and allows him to lead her out.*

SCENE SEVEN

The house site. Daytime. CHRISTINE *is measuring sheets of fibro, marking the shape with a carpenter's pencil, angle and rulers. She slips the tools in and out of her work pouch with familiar ease and speed. She scores the fibro and then snaps the sized pieces over a work bench. The baby, asleep in the pram next to her, starts to grumble. She stops to pick him up.* SUE-ANNE *lumbers up to the house. She's sulky and testy. She dumps a load of shopping—food and hardware—down in front of* CHRISTINE.

CHRISTINE: You look tired.

SUE-ANNE: Do your own fucking shopping next time.

> *The baby stops grumbling.*

CHRISTINE: He cheered up when he heard your voice. He knows your voice.

> SUE-ANNE *immediately melts into doting singsong.*

SUE-ANNE: Do ya, Clint? You know Mum's voice, doncha gorgeous? That's Mum's gorgeous boy... Ohh, my back's so bad. It's bad today.

CHRISTINE: Sit down. I've got him.

> *She settles the baby back in the pram as* SUE-ANNE *flops herself down. She's keen to cheer* SUE-ANNE *up, involve her in the progress of the house.*

Hot water soon. You'll be able to have a bath. Sleep in a real bed.

SUE-ANNE: Gary woulda had it done by now.

> CHRISTINE *turns back to look at the house.*

CHRISTINE: Yeah well, I dunno how Gary did half this stuff by himself.

SUE-ANNE: He was always rigging up contraptions and that.

CHRISTINE: Did you ever help him?

SUE-ANNE: One time. [*She smiles, remembering.*] This one time, he wanted to get this big bit of wood right up—

CHRISTINE: The ridge-beam.

SUE-ANNE: Yeah, whatever. Anyway, he ties this rope onto the wood and the other end onto the towbar on the ute. He gets me to drive the ute down the hill while he's climbing around up the top. He's yelling out to me 'Stop there!' and I go 'What?' like I can't hear him, even though I can. And he's going 'Go forward! Two inches! Stop! Jesus H. Christ, Sue-Anne, stop!' [*As herself*] 'What? What?' Jeez, he got riled up.

> CHRISTINE *smiles, enjoying* SUE-ANNE*'s story.*

CHRISTINE: But he got it up there in the end.

SUE-ANNE: I guess so.

CHRISTINE: It is very beautiful up here... But I don't see how anyone could make a living on this land.

SUE-ANNE: Oh no, Gary had it all worked out. He was gonna turn it back into a sheep farm.

CHRISTINE: Yeah?

SUE-ANNE: But Dave always reckoned there wasn't enough paddocks.

CHRISTINE: Did Dave say how much more land you'd need— (to run sheep?)

SUE-ANNE: [*irritated*] I don't know.

CHRISTINE *can see that* SUE-ANNE*'s mood is turning miserable and her back is hurting.* CHRISTINE *goes over to stroke her back soothingly.*

CHRISTINE: Want to come and see the new doors?

SUE-ANNE: I don't give a flying fuck about doors. Why did I ever think I could live in this shithole? Who am I meant to talk to? You and a few boozy old creeps at the pub.

CHRISTINE *is anxious to cheer* SUE-ANNE *up.*

CHRISTINE: Oh well, I'll ask Dave to come over for dinner. If we get him drunk, he'll make up some bullshit stories—give us a laugh.

SUE-ANNE *shrugs, sobbing.*

SCENE EIGHT

It's night. SUE-ANNE, CHRISTINE *and* DAVE *are huddled around the gas lamp in front of the house where they've just finished having dinner.* SUE-ANNE *is rugged up in voluminous blankets, holding the baby close.* CHRISTINE *is quite drunk—making her expansive and unguarded.*

SUE-ANNE: Other blokes prob'ly would've bullshitted me to get their greasy paws on my compo money. But Gary really loved me. I know that... Aww... feel a bit off my face. The new pills are making me feel spacey...

CHRISTINE: Lie flat then.

She makes space beside her for SUE-ANNE *to lie down, maybe with her head resting against* CHRISTINE*'s lap.*

SUE-ANNE: Gonna be so weird living here—just me and Clint. No one to talk to at night and that.

CHRISTINE: Look, Sue-Anne—I've said I won't leave until you feel okay to be by yourself.

This is news to DAVE. CHRISTINE *is aware that* DAVE *is throwing her a questioning look, but she refuses to meet his eyes.* SUE-ANNE *is getting whoosier.*

SUE-ANNE: Getting cold at night-time.

DAVE: Wait till July.

Meanwhile, CHRISTINE *is tucking the blankets up around* SUE-ANNE *with the unconscious gestures of a parent with a little kid.*

CHRISTINE: Ah well, they're demolishing a house out the back of Ken's place. Guy said he'd give me the pot-belly stove for ten bucks. Keep this house toasty warm.

She looks down to see that SUE-ANNE *has fallen asleep. Her grip around the baby is becoming precarious.*

[*Whispering*] Sue-Anne?

DAVE: She's out to it. Look out, Clint.

CHRISTINE *gently prises* SUE-ANNE*'s arms loose enough so she can rescue the baby from falling.*

CHRISTINE: Milky dribble's not a good look, mate. Let me... I'll just...

She wipes the baby's face with a corner of the blanket.

DAVE: Hey, Clint. Looking pretty hot now.

CHRISTINE: Admit you like them.

DAVE: They're nice little creatures.

CHRISTINE: More than that. He's got a good effect on people.

DAVE: Baby smiles at parents—'Ooh, isn't he lovely'. Parents feel better for a minute. Doesn't mean the kid's doing very well out of the deal. What if the parents are miserable screwed-up losers, all the smiling and gooing in the world isn't gonna save that kid, is it?

CHRISTINE *gently puts Clint back to sleep in the pram. Then she looks down at* SUE-ANNE *asleep.*

CHRISTINE: Maybe her and Gary would've made a go of it.

DAVE: And sometimes there's the stench of something doomed.

CHRISTINE: How come you're such a romantic, Dave?

DAVE: It looks to me like most couples fall for each other's worst features. They connect at the broken bits.

CHRISTINE: Ragged edges meeting up. Is that such a bad thing?

DAVE: Don't see it working out very often.

SUE-ANNE *snuggles up close to* CHRISTINE, *completely relaxed.* CHRISTINE *looks down at her and laughs.*

CHRISTINE: I've got a new month's resolution for myself. Don't let Sue-Anne rile me up.

DAVE: Waste of time getting cranky with a force of nature like Sue-Anne.

CHRISTINE: [*she likes this notion*] A force of nature. Except this one needs looking after like a little kid.

DAVE: Yeah.

CHRISTINE: How come I ended up lumbered with the childcare?

DAVE: Well… you know… I respect you for that.

CHRISTINE *is wary that he's taking the piss.*

CHRISTINE: Not that you'd be a mug like me.

DAVE: [*grinning*] No, I'm allergic to responsibility. You must be a better person than me.

CHRISTINE: [*laughing*] God, I've never been accused of that before.

DAVE'*s tone takes a deeper, more serious edge in the next lines. But at that same time, the baby stirs and* CHRISTINE *is momentarily distracted, cuddling him back to sleep.*

DAVE: Yeah well, if people took responsibility for what fell in front of them, maybe things wouldn't always have to turn out so shithouse.

CHRISTINE *looks up with a beaming smile.*

CHRISTINE: I gotta say—ha! I'm drunk… saying this 'cos I'm drunk—I gotta say, this feels good.

DAVE *smiles, shaking free of his grim mood, to see her so expansive.*

DAVE: What—you mean—?

CHRISTINE: [*indicating the baby*] This. I wasn't expecting it. I s'pose it's hormones. So human beings'll look after little babies instead of leaving them out on the savannah to perish.

DAVE: Don't ask me.

CHRISTINE: Anyway, there's all this joy built into it. It's taken me by surprise.

DAVE: Surprised by joy.

CHRISTINE: This morning I felt like—oh, you'll laugh at me. You'll piss yourself.

DAVE: I won't.

CHRISTINE: Yes, you will.

DAVE: I might not.

CHRISTINE: You will… but fuck it—there's no one else here to say it to. This morning, I took this deep breath and it was like I could get more air in. Bits inside my lungs have opened up and I can suck in more air. Laugh now.

DAVE: Sounds very pleasant.

CHRISTINE: Yeah but it sort of aches like the muscles are stiff. But yeah, it's a good feeling. Filling up with good feelings. Ha! Have you ever seen me this drunk and pathetic?

DAVE: Don't keep saying things like that.

CHRISTINE: [*scrutinising him closely*] You are one of those types that people confess things to, aren't you?

DAVE: Well…

CHRISTINE: People come up to you in waiting rooms and on buses and reveal all their secrets to you. I bet.

DAVE: I keep a good secret.

CHRISTINE: I can't believe how much I tell you, and you never reveal anything about yourself. I hate that.

DAVE: Well, I'm sorry. Ask me a question then.

CHRISTINE: I could ask you about your family.

He braves a smile, but his face is pinched and apprehensive.

DAVE: You could.

CHRISTINE: Nah, doesn't work like that. Oh, Sue-Anne left that lamp on again.

They both turn to see that a gas lamp has been left on inside the house. It glows through the windows, making the house look lived in.

DAVE: Looks like a real house. With people living inside.

CHRISTINE has kept her face turned away from him. He then notices that she's crying.

You all right?

She turns back, teary but smiling.

CHRISTINE: Yes, I'm okay... don't know why I'm crying... 'cos I feel fine really. I don't know...

DAVE *takes hold of her hand, stroking her arm, edging closer.*

This is so stupid... I don't even know why I'm crying.

DAVE: Don't worry about it.

CHRISTINE: I'm actually okay... I mean... this is...

DAVE*'s comforting embrace eventually turns into a kiss.* CHRISTINE *is taken off-guard and for a moment, they both let themselves give in to the kiss.* CHRISTINE *then pulls away.*

DAVE: What?

CHRISTINE: This is a bad idea.

DAVE: Oh... is it?

CHRISTINE: Bad for me anyway. This is where Christine could get pulverised.

DAVE: Come on, what kind of person do you think I am?

CHRISTINE: I might expect more. And you can't promise more, can you?

DAVE: Well, no.

CHRISTINE: So you'd better go home.

DAVE: If you call a garage next to a burnt-out house, home.

CHRISTINE: Well, you'll be flying out soon anyway.

DAVE: On the fifteenth. [*Indicating the sleeping* SUE-ANNE] Want me to carry her down to the tent?

CHRISTINE: No, I can. There's nothing of her.

DAVE *watches her gather up the empty bottles, preparing to go to bed.*

DAVE: Christine.

She steadfastly refuses to look at him. He reluctantly turns and disappears into the darkness.

SCENE NINE

The hardware store. VINCE *is consulting a list to gather the items* SUE-ANNE *is purchasing.* SUE-ANNE *is in full whingeing flight, with* VINCE *murmuring in sympathetic agreement to whatever she says.*

SUE-ANNE: She's a bully. 'Sue-Anne do this.' 'Sue-Anne go to tech and get your HSC.' She's got it all planned out, y'know. Well, fuck that. She's always screeching at me about Clint. He's my baby, isn't he?

> VINCE *nods emphatically.*

Just because she's a dried up old bitch with no bloke and no baby of her own, she's trying to take over mine.

> *He tuts and shakes his head.*

Sick, I reckon. Anyway, I'll go mental living up there with her. Know what I mean, Vince?

> *He nods earnestly. Her righteous, spiky tone suddenly dissolves into snivelling.*

Me and Clint need a proper life. Gary would've looked after us... I know that... What am I s'posed to do now? I need someone to look after me and Clint...

> *She flops onto the hardware store counter, sobbing.* VINCE *is astonished to see her there like that. He feels simultaneously terrified and compelled towards her. He gingerly reaches out a hand to pat her.*

Jeez, you're a nice person, Vince. You're the only person I can talk to like this.

> *Emboldened by her words, he tentatively moves his arm to enfold her shoulders. He clasps her hand, stroking it devotedly, holding on tight as if he's scared she'll run off.*

VINCE: I got another uncle with a cleaning business up the Central Coast. He'd give me a job. Reckon you'd like it up the Central Coast. Take little Clint to the beach and that.

SUE-ANNE: Yeah, being by the sea—that's gotta be healthy for babies, eh?

VINCE: My auntie'll help out with Clint and I can save up money for the deposit on a house.

SUE-ANNE: Might get my compo money soon—

VINCE: No, Sue-Anne. I will not touch one dollar of your compo money. I'll look after you and the baby and I mean it.

SUE-ANNE: Ohh Vince... I can't believe it. That's exactly what I want...

VINCE's earnest head-of-the-family tone suddenly drops for a grin of boyish thrill.

VINCE: Great.

SUE-ANNE: If there's really a God I reckon he sent you to me and Clint.

He squeezes her hand earnestly.

VINCE: I'm making you a promise, Sue-Anne. I mean it.

SCENE TEN

The house site. Daytime. CHRISTINE *is working at a frantic pace now, reminiscent of* GARY's *work frenzy.* DAVE *watches her. There's something unnervingly pumped-up about her heady good spirits.*

CHRISTINE: Celebration dinner tonight—reaching lockup.

DAVE: Congratulations.

CHRISTINE: How's it going with those buyers?

DAVE: Oh... yeah, nearly stitched up. That keen to get rid of me, are you?

CHRISTINE: No, I want to make an offer on your place.

DAVE: Eh?

CHRISTINE: I need to add your acreage to mine if I'm going to run sheep.

DAVE: You know bugger-all about running sheep.

CHRISTINE: I knew bugger-all about building until I started this.

DAVE: You haven't got any money to make me an offer.

CHRISTINE: Appointment with the bank tomorrow.

DAVE: They won't give you a loan.

CHRISTINE: They might.

DAVE: No way you could pay off a mortgage.

CHRISTINE: I've got some ideas.

DAVE: Come on, Christine, be realistic.

CHRISTINE: Are you saying you won't sell me your land?

DAVE: Course I'm not saying that. But this is a crazy idea and you'll
    end up—

CHRISTINE: What do you care?

DAVE: Well, I wouldn't like to see you end up in a mess.

>   CHRISTINE *turns to him with a wild-eyed smile, full of bravado.*

CHRISTINE: I quit my job yesterday.

>   *She throws her body into the work she's doing.*

I found out about tech courses. Sue-Anne can get her HSC and
then I'll help her do whatever she wants. No one else is offering
her that chance, are they?

DAVE: Guess not. But how long do you reckon she's going to hang
    around—

CHRISTINE: Does there have to be a time limit? Why can't this be
    permanent?

DAVE: Permanent?

CHRISTINE: Me and Sue-Anne and the baby. We can make that work
    as well as half the bloody normal families out there—

DAVE: Look, I'm no fan of normal families, but—

CHRISTINE: I knew you'd pour shit on this.

DAVE: What does Sue-Anne think of this plan?

CHRISTINE: You think I'm some madwoman with a crazy scheme.

DAVE: I'm asking you what Sue-Anne thinks.

>   CHRISTINE *refuses to entertain doubts—she just works more
>   feverishly.*

CHRISTINE: You don't believe people can make anything work, so of
    course you can't believe in this.

DAVE: Yeah, well—

CHRISTINE: It's easy to be chockful of wisdom when you sit around
    doing fuck-all. Easy to make no mistakes that way.

DAVE: Sometimes doing nothing can be the mistake.

>   *He is looking at the front doorway of the house.* CHRISTINE *is
>   too preoccupied to notice. She's spotted* SUE-ANNE *driving up
>   in the ute.*

CHRISTINE: She's got someone with her.

DAVE: Vince.

>   SUE-ANNE *and* VINCE *are holding hands as they approach her.*

SUE-ANNE: Me and Vince have got something to tell you.

She nudges VINCE *who's supposed to do it. He freezes with fear of* CHRISTINE. SUE-ANNE *rolls her eyes at his gormlessness and takes over.*

We're getting married.

CHRISTINE: Oh. I had no idea you…

DAVE *smoothly steps in to fill the gap left by the awkward reaction from* CHRISTINE.

DAVE: Congratulations, guys.

SUE-ANNE: Thanks, Dave.

CHRISTINE *decides she'll be happy too—gushy and frantic.*

CHRISTINE: Yes, congratulations! That's wonderful! We'll have to—uh—arrange—

SUE-ANNE: And we're going to live on the Central Coast with Vince's auntie.

CHRISTINE: What?

She is paralysed, sick—the ground has just collapsed underneath her.

SUE-ANNE: Leaving straight away atchally. I've just come to get my stuff. Where's Clint?

CHRISTINE: Uh… I put him down in the tent. You're taking him?

SUE-ANNE: 'Course I'm taking him. He's my kid.

She plays confident, but she is very nervous of CHRISTINE*'s reaction. She grabs the chance to march off towards the tent. For a moment,* CHRISTINE *is too pole-axed to respond.*

DAVE: Christine—

CHRISTINE: Sue-Anne! Wait a minute!

She runs off after SUE-ANNE. VINCE *winces apologetically to* DAVE.

VINCE: I'm sorry, Dave.

DAVE: Christ, you don't have to apologise to me, Vince.

VINCE: I'm sorry but.

DAVE: You don't have to apologise to anyone, mate.

VINCE: I love her. I really do. And Clint. I don't care if he's not my kid. I'll love him anyway.

Terence Crawford as
Dave and Ailsa Piper as
Christine in the 1996
Playbox Theatre Centre
/ Q Theatre production.
(Photo: Geoff Beatty)

Conrad Page as Vince and
Sophie Lee as Sue-Anne in
the 1996 Playbox
Theatre Centre / Q
Theatre production.
(Photo: Geoff Beatty)

DAVE: I know you will, Vince. But she's a handful. Are you sure you know what—?

VINCE: [*keen to have* DAVE *understand*] I know she's a handful. But I don't mind, you know? Because, like, people always reckon I'm a wet bastard.

DAVE: Hey, go easy on yourself, mate.

VINCE: No, I know it, Dave. A weak, wet bastard. But she needs me. She makes me feel useful. I like it, y'know?

DAVE: [*smiles generously*] I know.

> *He sees* CHRISTINE *coming up the hill after* SUE-ANNE. *Both women are tearful.* CHRISTINE *is frantic, panicking.* SUE-ANNE *is dogged, determined to go through with this. She pushes the pram, with a bag of her belongings tucked under one arm. She shoves the bag at* VINCE *to hold. She gathers up a few things scattered around the site.*

CHRISTINE: Just wait a minute, Sue-Anne.

SUE-ANNE: I said thanks for helping me out, okay? And I mean it.

CHRISTINE: Stop for a minute and listen to what—

SUE-ANNE: I'm doing this. So you might as well let me go without bossing me around.

CHRISTINE: I don't wanna boss you around—

SUE-ANNE: Don't make me say nasty stuff to you, okay? I don't want to.

CHRISTINE: Why is there a hurry?

SUE-ANNE: Piss off and leave me alone!

DAVE: Come on, Christine.

CHRISTINE: You stay the fuck out of this.

SUE-ANNE: Let's go, Vince.

> CHRISTINE *stands across* SUE-ANNE*'s path.* SUE-ANNE *snorts with disbelief, brazen but nervous.*

You going to try and stop me?

CHRISTINE: 'Course not. But I want—

SUE-ANNE: Leave me alone. Fuck off.

> CHRISTINE *makes a last plea, aware that it's ridiculous, but unable to stop herself.*

CHRISTINE: [*touching the edge of the pram*] Leave him.

  SUE-ANNE *wrenches the pram away from her.*

SUE-ANNE: Eh? I'm not gonna leave my baby with some mad bitch! He's my kid and he belongs to me!

  She flicks her head for VINCE *to follow and the two of them disappear offstage with the baby.* CHRISTINE *is frozen to the spot, gulping for air.*

DAVE: Look, Christine, I don't think—

CHRISTINE: Don't speak to me.

  She starts to circle, breathing hard.

DAVE: Hold on a sec… Christine…

  She grabs a sledgehammer and turns to the house. She gives the frame a huge thump with the hammer. She continues around the house and we can hear her taking out her anger on the building, with the sounds of the sledgehammer thudding down, glass shattering and timber splintering. DAVE *listens helplessly for a moment, flinching at the ugly sounds. Finally he goes after her.*

Christine!

  The two of them come back around to the front of the house as he tries to get the sledgehammer off her.

Don't do this.

  He folds her in tightly to him so that she can't swing the sledgehammer. The fight goes out of her with a sudden slump and she lets him take the sledgehammer.

Christine, listen—

  She pulls herself away from him.

CHRISTINE: There is nothing you can say to me. Nothing you can say.

  She flees. He watches her drive away and lets the sledgehammer drop from his hand. Then he walks away from the house too. We are left with the damaged, abandoned house for a moment.

SCENE ELEVEN

The house at dawn. It looks exactly the same as CHRISTINE *left it, with some damage and all the tools and materials scattered where they were. We can hear the sounds of the bush around the house but otherwise, it's silent.*

SCENE TWELVE

CHRISTINE *is in a motel room somewhere, talking on the phone. She is back in city clothes. She's got a bottle of wine and a TV remote control beside her.*

CHRISTINE: Well, I'm waiting to speak to the building inspector. No, no, don't put me on hold again, missy. You lost the call last time—

> *She sighs, cranky at being put on hold. She is trying to be brisk and businesslike throughout this call. The emotion sneaks up on her.*

Yes, hello. Yes, I know I spoke to you yesterday. [*Pause.*] I want to sell the property. [*Pause.*] No, my brother didn't put any plans into council— [*Pause.*] Don't speak to me like I'm a moron. I'm asking if your department can inspect the building and approve it retrospectively. [*Pause.*] I'm not going to be responsible for demolishing a perfectly good house— [*Pause.*] No, I am not getting shirty. [*Pause.*] Look, if you go up there and inspect it, you'll see it's a very well-built house. A solid house. [*Pause. She starts to get teary.*] I'm not getting upset—I'm angry. I'm bloody angry actually.

> *She slams down the mobile phone. She takes a deep breath and regains control of herself. Then she refills her glass with wine and turns on a TV with the remote. She flicks through the channels as we hear snatches of TV sound.*

The house is still apparently untouched, with no sign of life.
CHRISTINE *walks up towards it. She slows down the closer she gets,*
as if nervous of the power the house might have over her. She hears
a thump from inside and starts with fright.

CHRISTINE: This is private property!

> DAVE *appears around the side of the house, wearing a*
> *carpenter's tool belt.*

DAVE: G'day.

CHRISTINE: Am I having a vision?

> *He grins and shrugs.*

What exactly are you doing?

DAVE: Fixing up some of the damage you did. Didn't want to see all your good work get ruined.

CHRISTINE: I thought you'd have flown to the other side of the earth by now.

DAVE: Sale fell through.

CHRISTINE: Oh. Bad luck.

> *An awkward silence.*

DAVE: I heard in town you put this place on the market.

CHRISTINE: The money goes to Clint.

DAVE: Fair enough.

CHRISTINE: An inspector from the council's supposed to turn up this afternoon.

DAVE: Right. [*Nodding slowly, taking his time*] Well, I'm... uh... thinking of staying on at my place for a while and—uh—

CHRISTINE: Thought your parents' property was too small to be viable.

DAVE: Well... that's true. I was wondering if you'd sell me this place.

CHRISTINE: Oh I see. You're fixing up the house because you expect to live in it.

DAVE: No. No, that's not in fact why I'm doing this.

He keeps working as he talks, repairing something that CHRISTINE *had smashed up.*

There was a day—the week after you and Sue-Anne shot through—I was at my place. I heard this racket... where the kitchen used to be. Went to have a look and for a second I thought I saw my father—kind of wandering 'round the house like he used to do.

CHRISTINE: Been on your own out there too bloody long.

DAVE: Yeah. Anyway, it rattled me. So I came over here. And I looked at this house— [*His voice suddenly seizes in his throat, as grief has snuck up on him.*] I should've stayed with him.

CHRISTINE *is thrown to see him show such emotion.*

There was so much pain in Gary, it hurt to look at him sometimes, you know?

CHRISTINE: Yes I know.

DAVE: Felt like it was contagious or something. Everyone left him. All his life. Abandoned him. And so did I. [*His throat has closed up again. He tries to sound matter-of-fact and practical.*] Last week... I didn't know what to do. I looked at this house and there was some work to be done on it. So I'm doing it.

He looks directly at CHRISTINE, *appealing to her to understand.* CHRISTINE *opens her mouth to respond, but not sure what to say.* DAVE *smiles and flicks his head, letting her off the hook—he doesn't expect her to answer the unanswerable. He turns away to continue the job he's doing. It gets to the stage where he has to hoist up something heavy and awkward. On impulse,* CHRISTINE *steps in to help him with it.*

Ta.

Without either of them drawing attention to it, they begin working together, dividing the task with tacit co-operation.

So—uh—will you sell me the place?

CHRISTINE: You couldn't get the money.

DAVE: You got me there. I was thinking we could do some kind of deal.

CHRISTINE: What—one of those 'deals' where you get the land and don't pay for it?

DAVE: No. I was thinking of something more co-operative...

CHRISTINE: You mean like a merger?

He nods but doesn't dare look at her.

Put the two properties together in some kind of partnership—?

DAVE summons the courage to interrupt her with a direct appeal.

DAVE: Stay. Please stay.

SCENE FOURTEEN

Between scenes, we see DAVE *and* CHRISTINE *finish the house. They bring on plants to place around the house as if a garden has started to grow up.*

The house. It's a perfect brilliant day and the house looks like a fantasy happy home, with a neat little garden, pretty curtains and so on. The pretty stillness of the scene is broken by the raucous sound of SUE-ANNE *bursting out from the front door, nagging* VINCE. SUE-ANNE *carries an outdoor chair out into the yard. She is followed by* VINCE *who lifts out a stroller with the sleeping baby inside—Clint is now ten or eleven months old.* DAVE *gives* VINCE *a hand lifting the stroller over the front step but otherwise wanders down with them, unburdened.*

SUE-ANNE: I said to you—'Change the baby, Vince'.

VINCE: I didn't hear you.

SUE-ANNE: I practically screamed it in your ear, deadhead! Dave heard it over the other side of the room, didnya?

DAVE pulls a face—doesn't want to get involved. VINCE*'s response to* SUE-ANNE *is to be quiet and dogged.*

VINCE: I didn't hear you.

SUE-ANNE: You calling me a liar, dickhead? 'Cos I tell ya what—

VINCE: No, I'm not.

SUE-ANNE *groans with exasperation and flounces down ahead of him.* VINCE *doggedly follows with the stroller.* CHRISTINE *emerges through the front door. She is seven months pregnant. She carries a few more chairs. It's clear that* SUE-ANNE *has been getting on her nerves already.*

CHRISTINE: [*to* DAVE] Why in God's name did you think it was a good idea to invite them to stay a whole weekend?

DAVE: [*mock confused*] Ah—I thought it was your idea.

CHRISTINE: Bullshit. Anyway, how come you're the only person not helping to carry stuff down?

DAVE *grins—just his luck he supposes.* CHRISTINE *stomps down to join* SUE-ANNE *and* VINCE.

SUE-ANNE: Either you heard me and you're lying about it, Vince. Or you didn't hear me which means you're a deaf moron. Either way you're calling me a liar if you reckon I never said it.

DAVE: [*to* VINCE] So, how's the house going?

VINCE: Beaut thanks. Nearly there now. It's one of them kit homes but you get—y'know—optional extras and that—

SUE-ANNE: [*barging in, with childish excitement*] We got all the optional extras on the kitchen. Vince is a great cook. Just as well, since I can't cook for shit.

She guffaws loudly and we hear the baby yelp with fright.

Thanks a million, Vince. Thanks for bumping the stroller around and waking him up.

VINCE: I didn't bump the stroller.

SUE-ANNE: Wanted to have a minute of peace. No fucking way now, thanks to you.

VINCE *just sighs and lets it be.*

CHRISTINE: [*to* VINCE] Do you always let her talk to you like that?

DAVE *tries to signal to* CHRISTINE—*don't pursue this.*

VINCE: What?

CHRISTINE: I mean, you just sit there and let her treat you like a gormless nit—

SUE-ANNE: What? My husband is not a gormless nit! We all know you're a poisonous bitch. But don't take it out on my husband, okay Christine?

DAVE *puts his hand on* CHRISTINE*'s arm, quietly restraining her from biting back.*

CHRISTINE: I'm sorry, Vince. That was… mean.

VINCE: S'okay.

There's an awkward silence.

CHRISTINE: Dave's going out to spray the tussock tomorrow, Vince. You might like to go along.

VINCE: Yeah. Sure.

DAVE: I said maybe.

This is obviously a long-standing dispute.

CHRISTINE: Say so if you're not going to spray the tussock—because I'll pay Young Doug to do it. I can't do it like this.

She indicates her belly.

DAVE: I said I'd do it.

CHRISTINE: But I don't think you've quite grasped the difference between saying so and doing it.

She then notices that SUE-ANNE *is pulling conspiratorial faces to* VINCE *about* CHRISTINE *and* DAVE *spatting in front of them.* CHRISTINE *shuts up, embarrassed.*

DAVE: I actually love it when she talks to me like this.

CHRISTINE *smiles despite herself.* DAVE *runs a finger down her belly and she laughs.* VINCE *notices that* SUE-ANNE *has lit up a cigarette right next to the baby.*

VINCE: Put it out, Sue-Anne.

SUE-ANNE: It's my business.

VINCE: Next to the baby, it's not. Put it out.

SUE-ANNE: Piss off.

VINCE *just holds her with a stern look—he doesn't give up. She makes a great show of sighing and putting out the cigarette.* VINCE *then reaches out to grab her hand, stroking it, making sure she's happy again.*

Don't paw at me, Vince. Don't paw at me like some… little animal.

She flounces a few steps away and VINCE *waits patiently. The baby makes some noises.*

I knew it'd be like this. I knew I wouldn't get any peace.

Without the others seeing clearly, she fishes chocolates out of her pocket to placate the baby.

CHRISTINE: Anyway, Vince, we'll have to drive up sometime and check out your new house.

VINCE: [*grinning proudly*] Yeah. Lot of painting to do.

DAVE: Oh well, Christine's very good at painting.

He grins at her, teasing. She thumps him good-naturedly.

CHRISTINE: And Dave's very good at sitting 'round on his arse watching other people work.

VINCE *has spotted* SUE-ANNE*'s secret chocolate bribing.*

VINCE: Sue-Anne!

SUE-ANNE: What?

VINCE: We said no more chocolate!

The baby starts to cry at the sound of shouting voices.

CHRISTINE: You're pumping a baby with chocolate to shut him up!?

SUE-ANNE: He likes it! Now you made him cry, shouting at me!

CHRISTINE: If he fills up on garbage—

VINCE: He'll get fat and his teeth'll fall out and—

CHRISTINE: Exactly. Exactly.

SUE-ANNE: How come you two are ganging up on me? He's got a sweet tooth like me. Nothing wrong with that!

VINCE: Sue-Anne—

SUE-ANNE: Check it out, Dave! Ganging up on me and making my baby cry!

VINCE: Rock the stroller, Sue-Anne. Come on, he's upset now.

DAVE: Poor little bugger. All this shouting.

SUE-ANNE: Not my fault, is it?! I'll settle him down.

VINCE *gets up to grab the stroller from her.*

VINCE: Give him to me. There's a special way he likes it—

SUE-ANNE: Fuck off, Vince! I'll settle him down.

Meanwhile the baby's crying is loud and grating, getting more and more wound up. Sick of the baby crying and sick of the shouting and tension, CHRISTINE *snaps. She scoops the baby up out of the stroller and sweeps off towards the house with him, away from the others.*

Hey!

VINCE *yanks* SUE-ANNE *back to sit down, giving her a firm look—leave it.* SUE-ANNE *sulks but complies. Meanwhile,* CHRISTINE *takes up the even, loping gait of someone trying to rock a distressed baby into quietness. The baby's volume has dropped, but he is still upset and crying.*

CHRISTINE: Ssshh. Come on, little boy. It's okay now. Sshh. Come on. Settle down. Settle down. That's the boy.

She keeps up the soothing patter. Her rocking walk takes her closer to the front door of the house.

Look at that, little boy, some silly person left the front door open. Let all the flies in. I think it was me y'know.

She reaches out to pull the door closed. As she does so, the door swings open wider. GARY *is standing in the doorway of the house.* CHRISTINE *stands and stares at him, holding the crying baby. Then, on impulse, she hands the baby over to him. He pulls the baby in close to his shoulder, head cradled into his neck. He rubs the baby's back soothingly, drinking in his feel and smell. The baby settles into silence within seconds.* GARY *and* CHRISTINE *exchange a smile.*

THE END

www.ingramcontent.com/pod-product-compliance
Lightning Source LLC
Chambersburg PA
CBHW041931090426
42744CB00017B/2014